CMBS 911

ARE YOU READY FOR THE CRASH?

ANN HAMBLY

CMBS911
ARE YOU READY FOR THE CRASH?

ANN HAMBLY

1st Responder Publishing

CMBS911.com

Published by 1st Responder Publishing
CMBS911.com

ISBN: 978-1-7337236-0-2 (hard cover)
ISBN: 978-1-7337236-1-9 (soft cover)

Library of Congress Control Number: 2019903345

PRINTED IN THE UNITED STATES OF AMERICA
First Printing

Dedicated to the community of

First Responders everywhere

who dedicate their lives

to keeping us all safe.

"Ann Hambly is a professional's professional. Her first-hand decades of experience in CMBS servicing combined with her commitment to helping borrowers facing difficult situations is unequaled in CMBS."

– D. Michael Van Konynenburg, President of Eastdil Secured

"Ann Hambly knows the CMBS rules, structure and players as well as anyone I know. She has a passion for helping CMBS borrowers/ owners. Her knowledge, fueled by her passion, creates a winning combination for CMBS borrowers and owners."

– Patrick Sargent, Partner, Alston & Bird

"Ann Hambly has a vision. She believes in fairness, honesty and action, and has dedicated her life and her career to representing and guiding clients through the morass of regulation and pitfalls which often undermine the commercial owner's experience. Ann literally created a service niche to serve owners with CMBS debt. Ann very quickly became the Owner's lifeline. Ann is far and away the premier thought leader in her field and her book is required reading for anyone who is in the Commercial Real Estate market as an owner, broker, developer, or investor."

– John King, Cultural Architect, Renowned Author of Tribal Leadership

"As the captain of a fire department, my job is to save lives and add calm to a chaotic and oftentimes, life threatening situation. Although CMBS loans are not usually life threatening, Ann Hambly's role is that of a fire chief for CMBS. Her role is to add calm to the chaos and help owners save their properties and their financial investment. This book captures real-life life or death situations for owners with CMBS debt. I couldn't put it down."

– Bill Bathe, Captain, Tucson Fire Department, former MLB player

TABLE OF CONTENTS

INTRODUCTION

The Commercial Mortgage Backed Securities (CMBS) industry has an image problem.

Despite the fact that it can be a tremendously beneficial financial option for commercial property owners, investors, and the industry that serves them, it still occasionally suffers from a questionable reputation from what are now infamous deals gone bad.

If you've seen 'The Big Easy,' you know exactly what I'm talking about.

The industry as a whole can be complicated.

Sometimes confusing.

And more times than not, widely misunderstood and misrepresented *even by many in the financial services world.*

But I'm doing my best to change that.

Admittedly, it's not an easy concept to grasp at first pass. There are lots of twists and turns, rules (and exceptions to the rules), and allowances that can and *cannot* (or will or *will* not) be made depending upon an endless list of variables. No two clients have the exact same needs. No two investor pools have the same parameters, investment levels, and risk potential. And no two servicing arrangements present with the same mix of experiences, perspectives, and servicer inclinations. All of these variables frequently lead to a frustrating experience for the borrowers.

Every CMBS loan is different from the next one.

One of the most surprising aspects of the industry is often one of the most misunderstood aspects as well and it is often not realized by borrowers until *after* they begin having problems meeting the obligations of their CMBS loan. And the revelation? CMBS servicers serve one client above all others...*and it's not them.* Industry servicers' first and primary obligation is always to serve the investors whose funds make up the investment pool.

So, who does serve the borrower?

It's an industry with lots of different parties involved. And as is always the case when you bring together *any* group of people, they all bring to the table *their take* as to what they see as priorities. It's kind of like deciding who's going to bring what dish to Thanksgiving dinner. *Everyone* shows up with their own self-interests *front and center,* including their own expected responsibilities, self-perceived (or actual) limitations, preferable timelines, and personal motivations. If everyone's terms and conditions don't align, somebody gets upset and Thanksgiving is never the same again.

That's how it is for the parties involved in CMBS loans. Borrowers need relief. Servicers need numbers, analyses, proof of potential performance, and fees. Investors are looking for a promising ROI.

And everyone is concerned about the money.

With that in mind, the purpose of this book is to help you better understand one of the most misunderstood aspects of the commercial real estate industry—the processing and servicing of Commercial Mortgage Backed Securities, particularly from the perspective of the borrower/owner. My goal is simple: to clarify and identify the usual parties involved and their respective responsibilities, to explain the purpose behind each step in the process, and to give notice of what to look for *and steer clear of* in terms of professionals offering CMBS-related services.

As I mentioned, the process can get complicated and confusing.

It can be lengthy, complex, and discouraging at times.

But it doesn't have to be.

That's what this book is for.

Who Am I & Why the Fireman's Hat?

For much of my professional career, I have wrestled with how to answer the age-old question, "What do you do for a living?" It's obviously not a matter of *me* not understanding what my profession entails—because 30+ years in, I clearly do—down to the nth degree. But mention you're a 'borrower advocate in the Commercial Mortgage Backed Securities (CMBS) industry,' and the witty cocktail party chatter tends to come to a screeching halt.

People's eyes will glaze over as if you're speaking a foreign language.

They'll feign interest and nod knowingly as if they're familiar with the industry when, in reality, they haven't the slightest clue what you're talking about.

And they'll suddenly need to refresh their drink or have to make 'an urgent call' as a means of making a fast exit.

I get it. I really do. It doesn't easily roll off your tongue. Mention the word 'securities' and most people go 'all Madoff' on you, envisioning people in back offices making bogus real estate investments. Add to that, 'borrower advocate,' and it's just too many vague-sounding words for people to wade through.

And even though the industry has been around since the early 1990s and accounts for *about 10% of the* roughly $4 *trillion dollar*-commercial real estate market, most commercial real estate professionals have little more than a basic understanding about all that goes into a CMBS transaction. And for those that *are* deeply involved in CMBS transactions, their knowledge is usually limited to the scope of their specific services. In other words, they focus almost exclusively on the tasks that pertain solely to them and then pass the request on to the next service provider. Although they may do what they do very well, their involvement in and responsibility for the process usually ends when their requirements are met.

And even though the industry has been around since the early 1990s and accounts for *about 10% of the roughly $4 trillion dollar*-commercial real estate market, most commercial real estate professionals have little more than a basic understanding about all that goes into a CMBS transaction.

And so, after years of trying to explain the industry I've committed my entire professional career to *one more time*, it dawned on me...my industry—the world of Commercial Mortgage Backed

Securities—really does bear a lot of resemblance to a multi-car traffic accident...*in so many ways.*

I know what you're thinking...*"Who does that?* Who likens their profession to the nightmare of a dangerous automobile accident?"

Stay with me here and allow me to fully explain –

The more I thought about it, the more similarities I could identify. Not in the events themselves certainly, but more in the way both experiences are ideally handled—*through the coordination of lots of people, all with different areas of expertise, and all responsible for operating within an industry-wide set of professional parameters.*

Here are just a few of the similarities –

» Both industries respond to distress calls from people in very challenging situations. This means accepting the fact that people do irrational things and say irrational things when they're in very stressful situations. It also means servicers are also likely to be criticized most harshly by those that stand to lose the most. Whether crash victims or struggling borrowers, people are in situations they didn't necessarily volunteer for *and* that are frequently out of their control.

» Both industries have specific educational requirements and mandatory ongoing training to maintain accreditation. But arguably, for those involved in either profession, the most valuable training comes from on-the-job experience—the nitty-gritty, working-through-the-hard-stuff that serves to build a base of intuition and vast knowledge that comes only from exposure to many different challenges.

» Both professions can bring with them legal and ethical questions as to how situations are addressed and handled. Not only are servicers putting their personal reputation on the line every time they act on behalf of someone else, they're also representing their entire profession. The liability associated with each profession can be harmful personally and professionally.

» And lastly, both industries require someone to be passionate about their profession because, let's face it—there are much less stressful ways to make a living than pulling people out of banged up cars. Or dealing with layer upon layer of service providers with millions, if not *hundreds of millions*, of dollars potentially on the line. The emotional drain of serving people in these circumstances can take its toll.

Are you beginning to see how this unexpected analogy is starting to make sense?

To be clear, I don't for one-minute mean to equate a misunderstood sector of the financial world with the business of literally saving lives. Nor do I mean to imply the professionals in my field risk life and limb every day just by showing up for work as first responders are sometimes called upon to do. My honor, respect, and appreciation for those selfless souls within the first responder community runs deep. I am overwhelmingly grateful for their service.

So while CMBS transactions rarely involve smashed up vehicles, broken bones, and physical impairment, I still maintain there's a striking similarity between how their respective industries operate as well as the overwhelming sense of helplessness both crash victims and distressed borrowers experience.

And besides, this unexpected comparison between the two professions definitely captures people's attention long enough to actually hear "what I do for a living" at cocktail parties. And neighborhood get-togethers. And everywhere else someone has ever asked me, "C-M-B-*what?*"

> I still maintain there's a striking similarity between how their respective industries operate as well as the overwhelming sense of helplessness both crash victims and distressed borrowers experience.

And now the real similarities –

You know how it is when you come upon a serious highway crash involving lots of cars, maybe even a few critically injured people, and flashing red and blue lights *everywhere?*

It's overwhelming.

It looks beyond chaotic—*so many people* rushing around—some providing help, some *needing* help, and some, completely overcome by all that is going on around them.

And whether it's people or property or *both,* there is always *so much* at stake.

But allow me to let you in on one widely misunderstood fact:

Beyond what appears to be chaos and disorder,

there is actually a *highly calculated* order.

There is a hierarchy of service providers

and a systematic order of procedures.

Ultimately, however, in *both* industries,

one individual is charged with bringing order and calm to

the situation,

and with overseeing, coordinating, and triaging

the *most* pressing needs

to secure the *most* effective care

for those *most* at risk.

In the case of a multi-car collision, *that person* is the fire chief.

In the case of Commercial Mortgage Backed Securities (CMBSs), I am *that person.*

I am the fire chief.

Technically, the term is borrower advocate, but that lengthy label really just means I wear lots of different hats. It means I am the coordinator, the overseer, and the *one person*, in a field of many, who has a complete and comprehensive understanding of the whole process, start to finish.

And just like the fire chief at the scene of an accident, I am the primary advocate for the one most at risk—*the one who owns the property.*

After spending 30 years servicing every other aspect of the commercial real estate industry, I became acutely aware of a missing piece in the process of handling Commercial Mortgage Backed Securities—owner advocacy. It was a desperately needed, yet completely unmet need. My experience and insights were a natural fit for a neglected, yet substantial, population, *and I knew how to help them.*

As a result, I now focus specifically on helping CMBS borrowers who are either anticipating circumstances that would lead them to default on their loan or who are *already in the midst* of the default process. For years and years, I had watched as *the borrowers—* the very ones involved in *every single* CMBS transaction—were frequently at the mercy of out-of-touch lenders, uninformed handlers, and simply a lack of accountability from one processor to another. Most importantly, though, there was not a single person dedicated to looking out for *just them!* Simply put, the owners needed a fire chief to help them through the whole CMBS loan process because *they were the ones who had the most at risk.*

And that's when I decided to create the industry's

first borrower advocate company,

1st Service Solutions.

It is a calling I am passionate about—and that's a good thing, because the learning curve to grasp the constantly-changing aspects of a dynamic market is never ending. To become a truly successful borrower advocate requires a deep understanding of the entire CMBS structure, mastery of the different service providers' many rules, regulations, and mindsets, a far-reaching network of industry relationships, and a highly developed ability to think creatively when standard processes fall short.

It's not easy, but it is tremendously rewarding

It's like taking the Thanksgiving analogy a step further—to look at things from the perspective of the *one person* ultimately in charge of getting the whole meal on the table at the right time.

1

A CMBS PRIMER

To make sure we're all on the same page about the basics of the CMBS industry, I thought an overview of the industry, the processes involved, and the key participants would help to make sense of the details, the motivations, and the possibilities that come with *every CMBS loan*.

Virtually all commercial real estate loans are one of two kinds—portfolio loans or conduit loans. Portfolio loans require lenders to hold the notes on their books for the life of the loan. Conduit loans, or CMBS loans, allow lenders to sell their loans on commercial property holdings in order to free up their lending capital for other projects.

Here's how the process works –

In a CMBS transaction, individual commercial mortgages are pooled together and sold into a trust. The properties are typically diverse and include different size and types of structures in many different locations. They are usually a mix of retail centers, apartments, office buildings, and/or hotels. The pools usually include an assortment of 50-75+ diverse properties.

Once established, the trust acts as a 'conduit' or a pass-through entity also known as a Real Estate Mortgage Investment Conduit (REMIC). REMICs offer substantial benefits as long as they operate within the guidelines established by the IRS. These benefits mean they are not subject to tax, they can be highly leveraged to allow investors to minimize their tax implications, and they can issue a series of securities/bonds for investment purposes. Today, over 90% of CMBS transactions are treated as REMICs because of these significant benefits.

Upon the bonds' issuance, they are placed in traunches, meaning they are divided into various risk levels. This allows potential investors to select from a range of risk levels based upon the ratings determined by outside rating agencies. This process of converting commercial property loans into bonds and determining their respective ratings is referred to as securitization. Bonds are placed into one of three categories—investment grade, non-investment grade, and unrated. They are also ranked within each category.

Once the loan is operational, monthly payments on principal and interest are paid to investors beginning with those holding the highest-rated bonds. These investors receive their payments in full before lower-ranking, subordinate bond holders receive their repayment. This process of paying the highest rated to the lowest rated investors is known as the waterfall process.

For property holders electing to participate in CMBS loans, they are required to provide (or provide proof of) a 30-40% investment in a property's valuation, leaving 60-70% available for financing. CMBS loans are traditionally for a 10-year period with a fixed interest rate and with a large balloon payment due upon the loan's maturity. Prepayment penalties help to insure investors receive their anticipated return and discourage borrowers from paying the loan off early.

To bring all these properties together to create a single, highly desirable, investment instrument and to service it fully takes a tremendous amount of coordination and lots of personnel. There are government rules to abide by, preferred ratios of property variables to gather and maintain, and investors to appease. Once all the pieces, players, and properties are in place and borrowers can begin to meet their obligations, it can be smooth sailing for everyone involved. But when properties don't perform or economies take a downturn or consumer trends change dramatically, borrowers can struggle with crippling vacancies, delinquent tenant payments, and even their own inability to meet their financial obligations.

As part of every CMBS loan, there exists a team of industry professionals created solely for that specific loan. Though they are ultimately obliged to act on behalf of the investors, they can provide a starting point for borrowers seeking accommodations or loan revisions when problems arise.

The key players involved in most CMBS transactions, post-closing of the loan, include –

Primary or Sub-servicer – they maintain direct contact with the Borrower; this can be the loan originator or the mortgage banker who secured the loan;

Master Servicer – they service the loans in the pool through maturity unless the borrower defaults; they also manage the flow of payments and information and are responsible for ongoing action with the borrower;

Special Servicer – they are called in when a loan goes into default and are also responsible to the trust; frequently they are a related entity to the Directing Certificate holder;

Directing Certificate Holder/Controlling Class Representative (CCR)/B-Piece Buyer – they have an active role in monitoring the pool's performance as the investor in the most subordinate bond class and therefore, the one who will get hit with a loss when there is one.

Trustee – they hold all the loan documents and distribute payments received from the Master Servicer to the bondholders;

Rating Agency (ies) – they rate the securitization by establishing bond ratings for each applicable bond class and monitor the bond pool's performance to ensure the class ratings are equitable;

We'll go into much further detail on each of these providers including what I consider to be their emergency first responder counterpart in the chapters that follow. But for now, this general description is sufficient.

In the relatively brief history of CMBSs, much of the industry has continually strived to self-correct itself by closing in on loopholes in the process and working to eliminate collusion between servicers and investors. Many of these issues would not have even been discovered had it not been for the real estate collapse of 2008 which revealed a great deal of unethical practices going on behind the scenes. Prior to that, a booming economy and thriving real estate market had made it easy to hide mistakes and bad decisions. But when the wheels came off, so to speak, the many weaknesses widely exposed the need for tighter regulation and stricter monitoring. In the decade since, the industry has worked very deliberately to become more transparent throughout the whole process. As a result, the entire CMBS industry now has more clearly defined the rules, roles, and responsibilities for *everyone* involved. And yet, I still make it a priority to caution my clients to keep in mind the fact that the industry is still *unregulated* and unfortunately, some conflicts of interest still exist. There also exists far too many self-dealing and self-proclaimed freelancers that have taken advantage of unknowing borrowers in years past. For their part in addressing the problems, the IRS has since adopted a significantly heightened awareness in CMBS transactions. In recent years, particular attention has been paid to monitoring the industry's inherent conflict of interest and improper activities. They have also upped the ante in terms of accountability and the reporting requirements of CMBS servicers.

As a result of these stricter rules, CMBS servicers have become very cautious and rigorous in their processes, sometimes making the whole process seem as if it is an onerous, one-sided, and downright painful affair from a borrower's standpoint. Not surprisingly, these tighter guidelines and more closely followed procedures have also made it a bit harder to secure CMBS funding than in years past but, at the same time, have helped to better protect everyone involved—*even our national economy*—from repeating many of the same mistakes of the last major economic downturn.

A bit of oversight and some still-powerfully painful memories, it seems, has done the industry good, but there's still work to be done—*especially* in terms of borrower advocacy and reliable representation for them.

And that's where I come in...

FIREFIGHTERS &
BORROWER ADVOCATES
SERVICE ON THREE FRONTS

In addition to both emergency care crews and CMBS professionals bringing order to their respective areas of service *and* their industry-wide support of generally accepted best practices, they both are also traditionally called upon to serve in three distinct settings—as *preventative* advisors, in the handling of *foreseeable, but unavoidable* circumstances, and through their preparation for servicing *unforeseeable* emergencies.

At an early age, we learn of *preventative* practices from fire fighters and EMTs that serve us our entire lives. From Fire Prevention

Week in elementary school and the unforgettable "Stop, Drop, and Roll" jingle to later-in-life instruction on CPR, the Heimlich Maneuver, and the necessity of seat belts, we have all been exposed to some level of *preventative* steps we can take to be better prepared should an emergency situation arise.

Emergency teams are also widely known for the great lengths they go to in order to minimize the potential for pain and suffering when *foreseeable, but unavoidable* emergencies arise. Weather extremes such as tornadoes, hurricanes, flash floods, and snow storms are just a few of the emergencies they make provisions for in advance as a means of safeguarding the public. When everyone else is concerned with seeking shelter and safety for themselves and loved ones, it is the uniformed responders that weather the elements, answer SOS calls, and make the last-minute rescues of those who chose not to heed the preemptive warnings.

And in regard to handling the urgent distress calls of *unforeseeable* emergencies, these public servants are unmatched. Calls come in, people are hurt, lives are possibly at risk, and they know exactly what to do—first, for the immediate and most threatening need; and second, to minimize further injury. They get in, meet the imminent needs, and hand off the injured to more specialized caregivers, all the while working to restore normalcy to scene.

For those of us in the CMBS business, especially borrower advocates, we also do our best to service our clients in the face of these three situations as well. In terms of *preventative* measures, educating and informing past, present, and potential customers is our most effective action. By keeping abreast of market trends, economic shifts, and even in-depth analyses of trending consumer behaviors, we work to head off potential surprises for owners and advise them on potential, if not approaching, opportunities *and* setbacks. I consider it a vital part of my job to encourage my clients to also remain well-informed, especially in terms of the triggers in their loan documents as it relates to their cash management.

In terms of *foreseeable, but unavoidable* financial storms, I regularly go on the offensive and make many property visits and place even more calls to property owners. I share what I see coming and suggest next steps forward. Sometimes my words of warning are well-received and fully heard; other times, they fall on deaf, overly optimistic ears. My concerns are heeded much like it is when emergency responders warn people to leave town due to an approaching hurricane—some follow the advice, appreciative for the notice, and some choose to stay and take their chances.

Understandably, if I have an existing relationship with a client and share what I consider to be adverse and growing negative trends, they'll listen and take steps to prepare. If I don't have any kind of relationship with a particular property owner, my words of doom and gloom are usually not welcomed. Most of the time they'll thank me for my time but are quick to add, "Thanks, but no thanks."

"No worries," I tell them. "Keep my card, just in case."

They want to believe they're set for the time being. Their property is full, leases are signed and their tenants are thriving. Nobody wants to consider a time when it won't always be so. Life is good...until it isn't.

Life is good... until it isn't.

That was the case not too long ago with the nationwide closing of all the Toys R Us stores. From my perspective, the handwriting was on the proverbial wall. Their $5 billion debt was crippling, the big box stores and on-line retailers could meet or beat their prices and selection, and their massive brick-and-mortar locations were tremendously expensive to operate. After they filed for bankruptcy in September, 2017, I made appointments with several property owners with TRU stores. "It's Toys R Us," one owner told me, "they're part of America! They *can't* close the biggest toy store in the world!"

"It's hard to believe, I know," I commiserated. "but keep my card, just in case."

When the first wave of store closings occurred, it was all but over for the chain. They couldn't continue to do business under their current circumstances. Again, I made some calls and followed up on my first appointments. Looking back, the denial of one property owner was relatable, but it was still just that—*denial.*

"We're good," he said. "They're just closing down the low-performers. We're the only location for 15 miles. Plus, I can call my servicer when and if this happens and they'll work with me. Thanks, but no thanks."

"I understand," I told him. "but keep my card, just in case."

As soon as the announcement came that the company was closing down *all US locations*, suddenly *I* was the one getting the calls—*lots of calls.* The huge vacancies left by the mega-stores represented some serious *empty space* and *broken leases*—literally double trouble for commercial property owners. Their income was ceasing, but their property debt wasn't going anywhere and many property owners found out the hard way that the systematic way to handle these situations didn't usually include their servicers "working with them" in any manner they readily understood. Instead of offering suggestions, providing solutions, and good-naturedly understanding some events (like a nationwide store-closing) are out of a borrower's hands, the servicers were busy pursuing *their* agenda, working to do what was right for *their* customers (the investors, *not the borrowers*), and were talking terms and conditions that almost sounded foreign to their borrowers.

> The servicers were busy pursuing their agenda, working to do what was right for their customers (the investors, not the borrowers).

In terms of our accident scene, this would be comparable to an EMT calling in a "victim with an ALOC due to a self-inflicted GSW on BLS, arriving on a bus with an ETA of 4 to JPS." (That's code for a patient with 'an altered state of consciousness due to a self-inflicted gunshot wound on basic life support in an ambulance arriving at John Peter Smith Hospital in four minutes.') Even though the call makes perfect sense to the two parties involved, to the one who's actually hurting the most critically, they're unable to decipher what is going on all around them and what, if anything, is being done to help them.

As I said, I considered these closings and vacancies to be a somewhat predictable, yet unavoidable event. I couldn't control it or change the tide of consumer buying habits; all I could do was warn those who stood to be impacted the most, just as first responders do with expected natural disasters. Much like a fire chief warns their community of an approaching tornado, I shared the information I had available and offered a suggested plan of action. After that, the best I could do was to remain ready to answer their distress calls and show up prepared to help.

And then there's the *unforeseeable and unavoidable* challenges to the CMBS business. The events of 9/11 are an obvious example, but it doesn't take anything near as catastrophic to affect the CMBS market. Anything that adversely affects consumer confidence can, and usually does, have an impact on commercial real estate, especially if it continues for a significant amount of time. The declining value of the dollar, both at home and internationally, tense relations with other countries, threats of uneasiness on Wall Street, rising interest rates, and the changing dynamics of consumer shopping habits are just a few of the outside influences that can lead consumers to curtail spending, thereby reducing retail sales and profits. The immediacy of information, whether legitimate or speculative, can also have a big impact on overall consumer confidence.

While these outside influences can't be predicted or avoided, they can be managed, and preferably with a heavy dose of understanding for the individuals at most risk. That's where the human factor comes into play. Just as first responders have to address the practical, injury-related issues of an accident, most are also acutely aware of the human side of those they treat. Regardless of who's to blame for a traffic accident, the results are always the same—people are hurt and scared and in situations they didn't intentionally choose for themselves. As a result, most first responders never lose sight of the fact that *everyone* they treat is someone's child or spouse or friend and is *important to them.*

In my role as a borrower advocate, I also make sure to always remain cognizant that, beneath all the legalese and intimidating numbers, these are real people handling these transactions *and* carrying the debt. Decades of experience has shown me that a focus on both the dollar side of the deal *and* the human side is imperative for a successful resolution. For my clients, I work the logistics, coordinate the conversations between parties, and work diligently to pursue the best options for them. But I also go to great lengths to show my respect and appreciation for the service providers involved because I've been in their position as well. I consider it a priority to intentionally develop the trust side of the equation between both parties—*for everyone's sake.* Having been on both sides of the transaction processing, I can easily relate as few others can to what *both* are trying to accomplish. I am able to empathize with the servicers and am quick to give them credit for 'moving as fast as they can' even when much is out of their control. And I can equally empathize with the owners who are frequently facing threatening financial consequences. But no matter the circumstances, I never lose sight that there's truly a lot on the line *for everyone* involved in the business of modifying a CMBS agreement.

I am reminded of a time when a commercial owner, Kelli DiSabatino, called me desperate for direction and trustworthy help. She literally didn't know where to turn next to get the help she needed. She had a large CMBS loan that had matured and needed to be paid off *as soon as possible, but readily available refinance dollars were not enough to pay off the loan.* When she approached her Special Servicer asking for an extension, she was denied. She followed up with a request for partial debt relief, but was denied that too. She quickly concluded that she had no choice but to find some other creative source of financing to pay this loan off—even if it meant she was out of pocket a very large sum of money.

> Having been on both sides of the transaction processing, I can easily relate as few others can to what both are trying to accomplish.

Because she had invested so much into this property—a tremendous amount of time and money, lots of deeply personal sweat equity, and even tears—she was committed to not losing it. She located another lender who was willing to refinance her loan but sadly, her relief was short-lived. As soon as she asked her Special Servicer for a current payoff statement, she was shocked to see it included a late fee *on the entire principal balance* of her loan— almost $2 million—which meant that she didn't have sufficient funds to pay off her loan after all. All the work, worry, and stress of finding another lender only to find out the servicer had added another $2 million late payoff fee to her loan. It was defeating.

She was at her breaking point.

She begged the Special Servicer to waive the fee but quickly learned the Special Servicer's job is to get as much money as possible for the bond holders, which meant they had virtually *no incentive* to waive the late fee. By the time she contacted me, she was convinced she was going to lose the property. She was out of money, out of hope, and thought she was out of options.

"Ann was able to take the chaos of my CMBS loan and work through the myriad of details," Kelli explained. "I truly thought my situation was beyond hope, but she knew things a commercial borrower could literally never know and had the relationships with servicers to help me immensely."

Ultimately, it was a happy ending *on two fronts*.

As Kelli said, it was through a series of negotiations and some longstanding relationships that I was ultimately able to get most of the fee waived. This, in turn, allowed her to pay off her loan *and keep her property*. And just as important to me personally and professionally, it restored her faith in the processes and professionals within the CMBS industry and well beyond. "She saved my property," Kelli remembers, *"and my faith in others to help those in need."*

UNPACKING MY
AUDACIOUS CLAIM

L et me begin by unpacking my earlier broad-sweeping statement about the similarities between *the logistics* of emergency management and the CMBS industry –

Beyond what appears to be chaos and disorder,
there is actually a *highly calculated* order.
There is a hierarchy of service providers
and a systematic order of procedures.
Ultimately, however, in *both* industries,
one individual is charged with bringing order
and calm to the situation

and with overseeing, coordinating, and
triaging the most pressing needs
to secure the most effective care
for those most at risk.

Let's address the first part of that statement –

Beyond what appears to be chaos and disorder, there is actually a highly calculated order. There is a hierarchy of service providers and a systematic order of procedures.

Here's how –

What most of us interpret as chaos whenever we pass a catastrophic collision on the highway is usually *anything but unorganized or haphazard.* That's because firefighters and Emergency Medical Service providers (EMS) across the country all operate under one all-encompassing, *national* framework called the Incident Command System (ICS). The ICS is a highly thought-out set of policies and procedures intended to bring a consistent call to action and level of care whenever and wherever an emergency occurs.

By adopting the uniform guidelines of the ICS, both firefighters and EMS providers are better equipped to handle every possible kind of emergency situation they could ever face. The ICS provides a highly detailed chain of command, assigned responsibilities, step-by-step logistics, and more. First responders of all levels are charged with learning the common language and the shared terminology used by everyone within the emergency community for the sake of expediency and efficiency. This precise level of preparedness *by all responders* allows them to arrive at the scene of an incident knowing who is in charge, who to take orders from, and their immediate and direct responsibilities.

Just as a point of reference, the top five service providers in the chain of command of first responders arriving at the scene of an accident are:

» the Fire Chief

» the Assistant Chief

» the Deputy Chief

» the Battalion Chief

» the Executive Captains

One of the first things *all* responders learn is the importance of following procedures and honoring the chain of command. They are taught emphatically that when they operate within the boundaries of the ICS, they are kept safer and those at risk are treated more effectively. However, when individuals overstep their assigned parameters or act without the consent of the commanding officer, they oftentimes compromise both their personal safety as well as those they are called to assist. This behavior is called *freelancing* and can greatly interfere with, if not undermine, the operation's effectiveness.

"The guidelines of ICS are there for a reason," says Tucson Fire Department Executive Captain Bill Bathe. "People going off by themselves is what gets them killed. The case for following standard operating procedure can, quite literally, be a life-or-death decision."

Again, although the stakes in a CMBS transaction aren't anywhere near approaching life-or-death, to the owners of commercial real estate properties in times of distress, *it can sometimes seem that way.* Their livelihoods and financial reserves are often on the line as well as their professional reputations and relationships. The threat of potentially substantial and far-reaching negative repercussions also adds to the stress and anxiety of the mix.

Far more times than I'd like to admit, by the time a client comes to me for help they have oftentimes been misled or taken advantage of by so-called freelancing CMBS professionals who are either uninformed or ill-intended *or both.* When this happens, it can cost borrowers dearly in terms of time and money and even their faith in others' ability to truly help them. Uninvited or unauthorized freelancing on the trauma field or in the CMBS chain of command almost always has the same result—it harms the industry's reputation and, most importantly, the ones requiring the most urgent attention end up suffering more than they have to *now and later.*

Fortunately, just as there is a systematic order of procedures and a chain of command for emergency personnel responding to a crisis, there is also a widely accepted and orderly process that is followed throughout the CMBS industry. Like the ICS for emergency personnel, CMBS servicers must adhere to the Real Estate Mortgage Investment Conduit (REMIC) rules, the typical structure for a CMBS loan. REMIC is a creation of the IRS tax law that allows the trust holding the CMBS loans to serve as a pass-through entity, and therefore is not subject to tax at the trust level. Ironically, some of the seemingly nonsensical responses borrowers receive from servicers are the direct result of industry professionals working to ensure their compliance with REMIC tax law. Playing by the legal rules when it comes to REMIC requirements is extremely important to CMBS professionals, even if it means not always making sense to a confused borrower. Just like non-compliance within the ICS

Like the ICS for emergency personnel, CMBS servicers must adhere to the Real Estate Mortgage Investment Conduit (REMIC) rules, the typical structure for a CMBS loan.

framework can lead to disastrous outcomes, violation of REMIC tax laws can also bring about dire consequences for all involved in CMBS.

And like the emergency management process, commercial property owners are also best served when CMBS service providers respond quickly, use the correct protocol, and perform to the full extent of their responsibilities.

As a reminder, this is the hierarchy of the key players involved in most CMBS transactions, post-closing of the loan –

» the Primary or Sub-servicer

» the Master Servicer

» the Special Servicer

» the Directing Certificate holder/Controlling Class/B-Piece Buyer

» the Trustee

» the Rating Agency (ies)

Are you beginning to see how this unexpected analogy is starting to make sense? Allow me to wrap it up with my final comparison—*me*—*as the fire chief.*

The second half –

Ultimately, however, in *both* industries, *one individual* is charged with bringing order and calm to the situation, and with overseeing, coordinating, and triaging the *most* pressing needs in order to secure the *most* effective care for those *most* at risk.

Have you ever heard the saying, "Too many chiefs and not enough Indians?" Or maybe, "Too many chefs and not enough cooks?" They both mean the same thing—too many people giving orders can be disastrous in any setting. When people don't know who to follow, who to take direction from, and who is ultimately responsible for whatever the issue at hand is, it is ineffective at the least; and disastrous at the worst. This is true whether you're handling an emergency situation or needing approval on a CMBS loan modification.

One person has to be in charge and that person must know the proper process and protocol to follow.

One person has to make decisions based upon the circumstances as they present themselves *and* with the resources available at the time.

And *one person* has to coordinate the efforts of many.

This is where the similarities between my role as a borrower advocate and a fire chief *really* line up.

In the world of emergency management, decisions and directives have to become almost automatic to the commander in charge. There's not much time to consider every possible course of action and that's where a proven and systematic plan saves lives and minimizes damages. The following is just a glimpse into all that must be taken into consideration when emergency teams arrive upon the scene of an accident:

> "As an incident commander, when I arrive on a chaotic scene, I must quickly and efficiently survey the scene. Once I've gathered all the information that's readily available, I form a strategy and determine the tactics needed. I ask myself, 'What is the objective here and how will I implement it with the resources I have available?' This all happens *very quickly.* I then set up a command post and announce my strategy and objectives before beginning to make assignments to carry out my objectives. From there, I make constant assessments of how well these tactics are working and how well they are being carried out—it's a continual process until the objective is met."
>
> *–Bill Bathe, Incident Commander*
> *Tucson Fire Department*

Again, not that I deal with actual life-and-death scenarios, but every bit of what Commander Bathe outlined from the time he arrives on the scene of a disaster, with the exception of the very quick time frame, could be applied to how I take a struggling commercial property owner through the CMBS process.

Like the fire chief, my job as a borrower advocate also requires a heavy dose of 'big picture' thinking, a thorough understanding of 'who does what' throughout the entire process, a firm understanding of the REMIC tax laws, and a solid network of relationships with those who can be trusted to fulfill their responsibilities with accuracy and dedication to the property owner. And as it is with the chief, I take what I do very seriously and recognize the importance of reaching the borrower's objective.

When a client hires me, I also take a quick assessment of the circumstances surrounding their most immediate needs. I survey the scene, ask them where they hurt, triage where necessary, offer hope, and ultimately determine the best course of action. This is also where I ask myself, "What is the objective here and how will I implement it given the roles and responsibilities within the CMBS structure?" But unlike an emergency situation, my objective almost always remains the same: to help the property owner obtain relief from their pain, usually in the form of seeking a modification of their existing loan, and *always* with the ultimate goal of getting the best possible return for their asset.

Even though my objective remains consistent from client to client, the resources, roles, and responsibilities change with every borrower and every property I represent. Based upon the specific CMBS documents that govern their loan, every client presents with their own set of unique circumstances and needs. And this is where I am called upon to develop a unique and viable strategy with the tactics needed to reach the objective.

Lastly, for better or worse, the timing of when a borrower needs help can also play a significant role in the extent of the modifications servicers are inclined to make. As a rule, it usually follows that in times of thriving economic conditions, the process moves quicker and easier, much like handling a car collision on an uncrowded roadway on a sunny day.

Regrettably, the inverse is also true.

The outcome for a borrower needing modifications to their loan during tougher and tighter economic conditions can, and often does, deeply hinder the extent of the accommodations or concessions Special Servicers are willing to offer and accept. It is like needing emergency roadside care during rush hour on a busy highway in a snow storm—the prevailing conditions make it difficult to get the help that is needed.

But like the injured driver who didn't choose the time and date and conditions for the 18-wheeler to jackknife in front of them, a

CMBS borrower can face the same limitations. They can't predict or orchestrate trending economic conditions that affect their property's performance. Nor can they foresee their specific servicer's sentiment at the time they need assistance any more than they can change the weather. Sometimes you hit every green light on the way to work; sometimes it's nothing but red lights and detours.

The bottom line is this:

Timing is a major factor, if not *the biggest factor,*

in the breadth and depth of the help CMBS borrowers

receive in times of trouble.

But regardless of the prevailing circumstances *when* you have a wreck or when your CMBS loan comes due, the fact remains, when you need help—*you need help.* That's why, once my strategy and tactics are set and I've shared them with my client, I put my plans to work as soon as possible in order to ease their pain and calm their worries. And then an interesting phenomenon usually takes place. Time after time I've watched it unfold right before my eyes, and this is it –

When you offer someone a little relief or a glimmer of

hope and the comfort of knowing someone is dedicated

to helping *them and their situation,*

things can dramatically change—

especially when it seems all is lost for a troubled CMBS owner.

How it all comes together –

Just as I mentioned earlier how it sometimes sounds as if an EMT is speaking 'in code' when referring to a patient's condition, it is imperative in my role as a borrower advocate that I also know 'the code' and the shared terminology of my industry in order to be as effective as possible on my client's behalf. This can be a huge differentiating factor among borrower advocates!

When I begin to properly triage an emergency CMBS situation, I start with a review of the following –

»   the CMBS Pool documents

»   –to understand both the motives and investment levels of the servicers;

»   the Pooling and Servicing Agreement

»   –to understand the roles, responsibilities, and limitations of the various parties involved *in this pool;*

»   the status of the property

»   –to understand the issues currently at hand, its current and anticipated future value as well as an expected timeline to recovery;

»   the status of the property owner

» —to understand their motives, abilities, and inclination to work towards saving the property *or not;* in other words, do they want to retain the property at all cost or are they more concerned with the tax consequences or future borrowing ability if their loan goes into default?

And these are *just the beginning* of all that is involved in assessing a property's status *before* I can even consider getting to work.

There is almost always a lot to consider in any type of urgent situation—be it on the interstate highway or assessing the failing financials on a once-thriving shopping mall. Tensions run high and long-term outcomes remain mostly uncertain. Those hurting the most can't help but go to a worst-case scenario.

But then help arrives…

People are called in to assist and sort through the chaos. They know *what* to do first, *who* to help first, and *how* to help best. They're trained and experienced; calm and encouraging. And probably most importantly, they can see past the immediacy of the problem and onto a best-case outcome.

And best of all, *for all concerned,* they don't hesitate to jump in and get about the business of making it happen.

911 AND THE MASTER
SERVICER...THE FIRST
LIFELINES

ave you ever found yourself playing Santa at 2 a.m. on
Christmas morning going on your third hour of putting
together a couple of bikes and a full-size trampoline? Your Christmas
spirit has long since left you and there you are—surrounded by *lots*
of bolts and screws and industrial-strength *springs*, three *'easy-to-
understand'* instruction booklets obviously written by engineers,
and kicking yourself for not opting to spend a little bit more to get
the already-assembled versions of each.

You can actually remember the moment in the store when you brought all this on yourself—the moment when you made a conscious decision thinking, "How hard could it be? After all, isn't this kind of a rite of passage as a parent?"

"I got this," you told the guy working the toy department.

"Just be careful with the trampoline," he warned. "Sometimes they can be a bit tricky connecting the last few springs—especially by yourself. But, we'll be making house calls 'til 8 p.m. on Christmas Eve if you decide you need help."

"No worries," you said. "I think I can handle it."

Why do we do *that* to ourselves—take on jobs and tasks *well outside our wheelhouse* when there are people who can do it better, quicker, and without leftover plastic bolts and screws?

Is it the DIY culture that has swept the country? Have all the slick home improvement shows made *every single thing* look so doable. And simple. And affordable. "Don't pay a contractor," they say. "Do-it-yourself! And be sure it's done *right!*" Sure, it's easy when a prep crew has come in, measured and cut everything, teed it up to put together in three simple steps, and has a back-up set of supplies in case the first attempt doesn't end up looking entirely 'camera ready.'

Or maybe it's the false sense of empowerment we get from information gleaned on the internet that makes us think *absolutely nothing* is beyond our scope of understanding or doing or fixing *ourselves*.

Ever Googled your symptoms before going to the doctor and then showed up to your appointment confident of your *obvious* diagnosis?

> Maybe it's the false sense of empowerment we get from information gleaned on the internet.

Need to put-together a last-minute will for Grandma? There's thousands of templates, forms, and 'legal consultants' (whatever that implies) *on line* that can make that happen *in minutes*.

Or maybe you want to chart the course for your bucket list sail around the world? Somebody's been there, done that, and posted it on YouTube.

Mom and Dad were right…you pretty much can do anything you want…*sort of.*

No doubt, you can find virtually any and everything you need to know *on line* to some degree. You can also find a tremendous amount of false information, too. Some of it is naively posted by ill-informed people who are simply perpetuating second, third, and fourth-hand information about everything from alternative medical treatments to questionable investment advice. Sadly though, some of what you find online is maliciously posted by those wanting to take advantage of unsuspecting or overly-trusting individuals who subscribe to the idea that if it's on a reputable-looking website, it must be correct. There's an abundance of both the reputable *and* the shady for just about everything you can dream of searching for— from auto repair to open heart surgery (yes, unbelievably, there are step-by-step videos instructing one how to do it!).

But if you're needing to have the details of something significant, such as a catastrophic car wreck or a multi-million-dollar commercial loan, fixed, repaired, or resolved, there comes a point when knowledge (legitimate *or otherwise)* will only take you so far. *Now* is not the time to preemptively try to handle all the moving parts of an emergency situation nor is it the time to undertake the many levels of your CMBS-structured loan *on your own.*

Now is when you need trained, experienced specialists who do what they do so well, it is second-nature to them.

Now is the time to call for help from individuals who are unphased by the circumstances of your situation because they've heard it all and seen it all before.

Now is the time to allow specialists with a sense of perspective who can see past the desperation and emotion of your call and quickly size up the most pressing needs of *your* situation.

Now is time to enlist help!

When you need emergency medical help, you call 911.

When you need help or relief on your CMBS loan, you call the Master Servicer.

Both know *who* to call for further help.

Both know *what* questions to ask of *you*.

And while they are both limited in the scope of services they are personally allowed to provide, most of the time just making contact with them is enough to offer some degree of comfort because you know others are rallying to help you.

And that's just the start of the similarities.

Far and away the greatest similarities between 911 operators and Master Servicers lies in their need for relevant, actionable, and current information about your most urgent needs in order to determine how they can best serve you.

In both cases, the timing and details you provide about your situation are the crucial factors.

Let me be clear, whether medical or financial,—it is *always* best to make the call for assistance *as soon as it becomes apparent* you need help. No one trapped inside a mangled-up car ever got better by waiting to notify the authorities. Likewise, no borrower has ever done themselves any favor by allowing their loan to become severely delinquent and begin accruing penalties and interest with *every passing day before reaching out for help.*

To complicate matters a bit in either scenario—a physical emergency or an approaching need for revisions to your commercial loan—there's also the additional burden of discretion on the part of the caller and it comes with this caveat—***what you say is oftentimes as important as when you say it.*** That's because, *whenever you call and whatever you say to* both 911 operators and Master Servicers, they are obligated to *act on your behalf* and begin notifying all the appropriate parties once you make the call. And this *always* entails both operators and servicers keeping exacting, sometimes incriminating, records of *what you tell them.* This is *extremely* important to remember, whichever call you are making, because both scenarios can bring with them long-term and life-altering consequences simply based upon *what you tell them.*

The 911 Side –

The biggest complaint among 911 operators?

People who call them with non-emergency situations and random questions.

Most operators will attribute these types of calls to two primary reasons: ignorance or laziness—either the caller genuinely does not know whether theirs is an emergency situation or not, or more likely, they just didn't know who to call to help determine if they truly needed emergency assistance. And then there's laziness—calling for traffic and/or weather conditions, first aid instruction, or something even more removed from being an actual emergency, like the number for the local pizza place.

If your house is on fire or there's an intruder in your home, a call to 911 is obviously warranted. But in other, less clear-cut situations, it is not always so obvious. According to the guidelines of the National Emergency Number Association, also known as the 911 organization, the general rule is to "dial 911 any time there's a threat to life or property—such as an accident, a crime, a fire or a medical emergency...but when in doubt, always call."[1]

The organization's Education Director, Ty Wooten, explains far too many people still continue to remain unclear over what constitutes a *real* emergency. As a result, the number of 911 *non-emergency* calls each year has grown exponentially through the years. Ask a few veteran operators about some of the most absurd and useless calls they've received, and *every* operator who has logged more than a couple of years of service can immediately call to mind some of the most ridiculous calls they've received.

Burned the Thanksgiving turkey? Call Butterball; *don't call 911.*

Worried about an approaching thunderstorm? Watch the weather or check your local radar; *don't call 911.*

Need an argument settled? Google it, but *don't even consider calling a 911 operator* to resolve your dispute.

Legitimate emergency or not, every call to 911 is taken extremely seriously. Prank calls and intentional hang-ups are not tolerated well because they have the potential to tie-up resources that could otherwise be used to serve actual emergencies. Not only do prank calls take officers and equipment away from 'real' emergencies, but several bogus calls to 911 in recent years have even led to tragedies themselves including unnecessary deaths and 20+-year prison sentences for the malicious callers.

Across the board, operators stress the need to complete a call to 911 even if—*especially if*—you dialed them in error. Tell them it was a 'butt dial' or your kid messing with your phone—they'd much rather know it was unintentional than assume you need emergency assistance. Otherwise, *they'll call you.* And should you choose not to answer their call, don't be surprised if a police car or fire truck shows up from wherever your call was made. They don't joke around when *you call them* because operators never know if a call or hang-up is accidental or an intentional call in an active situation where the caller is in danger but unable to speak.

If you've ever called 911, you know the first thing the operator will ask is, "What is your emergency?" They need to know the nature of your emergency so they can best know who and what and how many responders and vehicles to dispatch. Understandably, the call-out for first responders differs widely for an active house fire versus a strange sound you may have heard outside your bedroom window— one requires all types of emergency personnel and equipment, the other probably nothing more than a routine perimeter check by a patrol car. But whatever the nature of a call to 911, *in every call,* the more accurate and relevant details a caller can provide, the better suited the manpower and vehicles sent to resolve the emergency.

A large part of this information-gathering process involves operators following a prescribed flow chart of questions designed to clearly establish what kind of help is needed, where the emergency is, and other, potentially helpful information including whether the emergency is still ongoing, such as an active hostage situation, whether weapons are present, and other possible threatening circumstances nearby. Vetting the extent of the information a caller provides is crucial to responding accurately and appropriately.

All too often 911 callers become frustrated or scared or panicked as operators continue to ask questions about the circumstances of the emergency. Operators are frequently told to, "Just send HELP!" as the caller's anxiety level rises. But as one veteran operator explained, "Believe me, we're not fishing for juicy details to share later in the break room; we're simply working through a systematic approach designed to gather *the most pertinent information available at the time of the emergency.*"

Most operators follow the guidelines related to the six W's –

» *What* is your emergency?

» *Where* are you reporting from?

» *When* did your emergency occur?

» *Who* is at risk?

» Are *weapons* present?

» *What* is the welfare of those involved?

When callers elaborate and want to explain every last detail, it not only slows down the operator's ability to get them help as soon as possible, it can sometimes unknowingly provide incriminating details—even those that led to the emergency itself. And every word is recorded. And allowable in court. And can be used against *you*.

Even when you don't mean to call them.

That was the case when a man in Hot Springs, Arkansas unknowingly dialed 911 while he was bragging about local areas thefts he had pulled off *while he was making a deal with his meth dealer!*

"It's definitely one of the stranger things I've seen in 18 years as a law enforcement," said Hot Springs Police Department Corporal Joey Williams.[2] Needless to say, the conviction stuck.

Even though callers frequently forget they are talking to operators and *not physicians* in the heat of the moment, 911 operators are bound by a legal and ethical limit to the extent of aid they can render. Beyond the logistics of childbirth, CPR, and basic first aid practices, 911 operators are not trained to provide much further medical advice, *even if they want to or know how to.* Again, their job is about one primary thing—gathering as much relevant information as possible and relaying it to those who can take the situation from there.

The Master Servicer Side –

Just as the call for help in a threatening or physical emergency begins with a call to 911, a commercial borrower in need of temporary relief on their payments, revised loan terms, or the more extreme need to reduce the debt, should begin with call for help to their Master Servicer. They are the first line of support for a borrower in good times and bad—*especially in the midst of or anticipating circumstances* that will prevent them from staying current on their loan.

As long as a you continue to be consistently able to meet the terms and conditions of your loan, all questions, cares, and concerns regarding your debt's maintenance and status are fielded by your Master Servicer. As an overview, these are the traditional responsibilities most Master Servicers provide –

» they collect and process payments and oversee the collections account which holds funds;

» they compile lots of loan information; as the primary clearinghouse for the overall CMBS transaction, they collect periodic operating statements and rent rolls and maintain the records for payments received;

» they inspect properties at least annually, though often more frequently, to confirm property conditions are as reported and/or to note areas requiring attention;

» they oversee the records for property taxes, other costs, escrow accounts, and necessary insurance; they must be able to report and verify adequate insurance is in place as well as sufficient escrow or reserve accounts to cover taxes and insurance premiums.

Should circumstances arise where you find yourself unable to continue making timely payments or anticipate becoming so, it is important to contact your Master Servicer with an understanding of the extent to what they can do for you. Remember the limitations placed upon 911 operators regarding the services they can render? Master Servicers are also limited by highly restricted terms of actions (primarily the REMIC tax laws) they can *personally* take on your behalf as a borrower. But again like the 911 operators, they *are the correct and crucial first call to make* because *they can initiate the process* to get help for you.

But let's assume you are truly in need of some financial wizardry to see you through a setback and you're preparing to make *the call.* What now? Gather your financial statements and get in contact with your Master Servicer as soon as it becomes apparent you will be unable to honor the terms of your loan for much longer. There's even a term for this prime window of opportunity for seeking restructuring assistance and it's called *the Golden Hour.* And, not surprisingly, the same phenomenon exists in actual emergency situations as well and is called the *same* thing. In both situations, the Golden Hour is a brief and fleeting time frame when seeking and receiving the appropriate help is most beneficial, where it can mean the difference between a borrower maintaining financial solvency or a patient living to tell about their experience. Because stories about the Golden Hour in both emergency situations and

There's even a term for this prime window of opportunity for seeking restructuring assistance and it's called the Golden Hour.

financial crises are so legendary, we'll further explain just how crucial it is to call for help *as early as possible* in a later chapter.

Getting the Wheels in Motion –

In CMBS transactions, the Special Servicer is *the only one* who can modify a loan. And here's where it gets tricky. And confusing. And frustrating for the borrower because a borrower cannot speak to the Special Servicer unless their loan has been officially transferred *to the Special Servicer* by the Master Servicer. Add to that the fact that there are only two ways a loan gets transferred—through an actual default, indicating two or more payments have not been made, or if an *imminent default* is likely to happen. *As far as it is possible,* it is always preferable for the loan to be transferred to the Special Servicer *before the actual default* takes place.

Put it this way—say you're curious about visiting your county jail—you know, what it's like, the conditions, is it really like how it is on TV and in the movies. Is it like Mayberry or Alcatraz? There are two basic ways to get there: call City Hall and make arrangements for a tour *or* drive 75 mph through a school zone with a suspended license and no proof of insurance. Either way will get you a tour, though for the later, you may not be allowed to leave without posting a large bail. Likewise, going to the Special Servicer *proactively* will also serve you better in terms of how your need for assistance is considered by those in the best position to help you.

When a distressed borrower makes a preemptive call for help to their Master Servicer, it is actually a call *for the Master Servicer* to call upon the Special Servicer to help, just like calling 911 is the first send-up for emergency help. And again, just as callers can sometimes become frustrated, scared, or panicked as operators continue to ask questions about the circumstances of the emergency at hand, commercial real estate owners frequently also go through many of the same emotions. In both cases and as anxiety levels rise, callers want to bypass all the background information and resort to yelling, "JUST HELP ME!"

And finally, just as 911 operators are not the ones actually providing the emergency help, a Master Servicer *also* doesn't render *the actual help* either but they also are required to work through a systematic process that helps them *gather the most pertinent information available at the time of a borrower's emergency.* To do so, most Master Servicers ask these questions as part of their initial assessment of a borrower's financial standing –

> » *What* is your emergency or current situation?

> » *When* did your emergency occur?

> » *Will* you be able to continue to making payments?

The same rules for brevity of details and explanations when calling 911 also apply when a borrower makes the initial call for help to their Master Servicer. A borrower's first call for assistance is not the time nor the place to offer a suggested plan of resolution. When borrowers want to explain every last detail, it not only slows down the Master Servicer's ability to request help, it can also lead to a caller unknowingly providing incriminating details that led to their emergency situation in the first place! Like the distracted mom charged with criminal negligence when her unsupervised child drowns, every word you share is recorded, allowable in court, and can most definitely be used *against you.*

> A borrower's first call for assistance is not the time nor the place to offer a suggested plan of resolution.

As it is when calling 911, if you are a *currently or potentially distressed* borrower, you need to be very specific about what you need most. As a CMBS borrower facing threatening circumstances, you are calling *for your loan to be transferred to the Special Servicer.* You don't have to explain what YOU plan to do to fix the situation or what you have done to-date to try and fix it; *all you need* is for the appropriate person to be notified that *you need help.* And here's the ironic twist to it all—before your Master Servicer begins the process of transferring your loan to the Special Servicer, *they* must first be convinced that there is a legitimate need for help.

Sounds counterintuitive, doesn't it? *You have to convince them* you're fast approaching default status and *they're the ones in danger* of not receiving complete repayment for the monies *they loaned you.* Shouldn't that be a serious concern *to them as well?* As is usually the case, there's a backstory that explains what appears to be backwards thinking...

After the collapse of the real estate markets in 2008 which led to a national recession, stories of tremendous concessions being made by lenders to overburdened borrowers became legendary. And all it took was for a few people in the early months of the financial tsunami to share *their* fortunate restructuring arrangements with *their* friends and the snowball effect of concession-seeking borrowers picked up some serious momentum. Word spread fast and opportunity-seekers moved in even faster and all with the same rationale—"I've got more debt than they do! If their lender gave them a discounted payoff, I'm all in to do the same!"

Any of that sound familiar? Like maybe a childhood memory when you first came to understand the concept of 'the squeaky wheel gets the grease?' Or maybe the time when your brother got a popsicle for 'being good' because he went and bragged to mom and you were overlooked even though you hadn't hit your sister for three whole days. Suddenly, you felt compelled to tell mom just how good you'd been, too, and before you knew it, you were licking red sticky syrup off your hands and chin too.

If somebody else gets a deal, and the chance to make their life a bit easier, we want the same deal too—whether we're deserving or not. That's exactly what happened in 2008-12 when lenders tried to put a tourniquet on the hemorrhaging of loan defaults as the fallout of a recession trickled down to end consumers and their evaporating disposable income. Initially, observant borrowers in legitimate need of debt restructuring were granted concessions and allowances and modified terms. But when word got out about the accommodations being offered in an effort to steady the rising tide of defaults, even many borrowers who were still financially soluble wanted their piece of the pie of the generosity accommodations, too. An epidemic case of "I'll have what she's having" hit the lending institutions of America swiftly and forcefully.

As a means of slowing down 'the concession bandwagon,' lenders tightened the threshold for making allowances and lessened the grace granted to borrowers looking for debt relief. Since then, the onus for making a case for debt assistance has been placed squarely on the shoulders of borrowers to prove their need for assistance. You can't just *want* easier loan terms, you have to genuinely *need* them. And be able to prove it, too.

In terms of our first responder analogy, this would be like calling 911 just because you stubbed your toe really hard on the nightstand and wanted an ambulance to come check it out. Sure, it hurt like heck, and it might even be a little sore for a few days, but when 911 operators are fielding life and death calls for *real* emergencies, there's little chance that time, effort, and city resources will be wasted on your run-in with the furniture.

Calls to both 911 and CMBS Master Servicers operate on the same general set of terms–

Real emergencies warrant real emergency assistance;

but temporary inconveniences and minor difficulties

are best handled with a shot of fortitude.

Once a Master Servicer agrees with a borrower that their loan needs to be transferred to the Special Servicer, the process begins. The first step, the actual transfer, occurs through an official Letter of Imminent Default, followed by a series of events which we will explain in detail the following chapters.

Remember, as a borrower needing help, *how* you go about seeking resolution should always be tempered by what you say and what you *don't* say because it can dramatically affect how your financial emergency is handled. Distressed CMBS borrowers are well-advised to choose their words carefully when making a request for their loan to be transferred to the Special Servicer when requesting an imminent default letter. There's a huge difference between telling your Master Servicer you *can't* make your payments versus you *won't* make your payments. Although it sounds like little more than semantics, the difference is extremely important.

In what turned out to be a major court case, precedents was set regarding the importance of exactly *what a borrower tells their Master Servicer.* Because CMBS loans are non-recourse, meaning that, in the event of a default, the only recourse available to a lender is the actual property and not the sponsor personally, it makes CMBS loans very attractive to borrowers. However, there are some exceptions to this, affectionately referred to as 'bad boy carve-outs.' In layman's terms, these 'carve-outs' allow a lender to seek repayment from the actual individual owner(s) when/if the owner maliciously does something that causes the property to lose value. A common 'bad boy carve-out' violation occurs when the owner files bankruptcy just to stop the lender from taking ownership of the property.

In more obscure violations, sometimes it even comes down to the owner's insolvency that is at issue. In a well- known legal case in the State of Michigan in 2011, the court ruled that an owner presenting his inability to pay outstanding debt triggered the case for the *insolvency* 'bad boy carve-out,' thus allowing for full recourse of the loan. Since then, years of legal wrangling have gone into the interpretation of the implications of insolvency claims. As a result, commercial borrowers should always be intentional in terms of *exactly what* they say when presenting a need for assistance, being careful to never state they *'can't make their payment,'* but that they *'won't make their payment.'* It seems a minor distinction, but it can bring with it potentially very large consequences.

When you really think about it, that's not too far removed from the weary parent being *unable* to put the Christmas Eve trampoline together compared to

> The difference of a single word—**can't vs. won't**—can make all the difference.

the overly-confident parent simply choosing *not* to put the effort into making Christmas wishes come true. In the first case, Dad is just a tad bit too inept to master the assembly instructions; in the other, he's intentionally willing to risk the disappointment of his kids' Christmas wishes because he doesn't want to put forth the effort.

Sure, that's a simplistic example, but it makes the point of how the difference of a single word—*can't vs. won't*—can make all the difference in the world on Christmas Eve or any other day.

EMTS AND SPECIAL
SERVICERS

❝❝Give me an ABG, CBC, chem 7, cardiac enzymes, and coag panel…"

Sound familiar? It's the battery of tests most television emergency room docs rattle off as soon as a seriously injured patient arrives at their fictitious ER. I've heard it so many times, I think I could order the tests myself. And I'm not alone—by a long shot.

Television network execs have long since known we have a collective curiosity about the trauma and drama that goes on in a metropolitan emergency room. Sure, most of us have been to the ER a time or two maybe as a kid with a broken arm. Or as a college kid injured in a dare taken too far. Or even as an adult possibly trying to relive our 'glory days' back to a time when age wasn't fighting against us. But because most of us haven't experienced a life-or-death situation during our personal ER visits, collectively we remain intrigued by the overly dramatic ways big city hospital emergency rooms are presented in movies and on television.

In fact, the formula has such a proven track record of success, networks have applied it almost since the beginning of television itself. See if you don't agree...

Think of your favorite 'trauma drama' –

George Clooney's early days in *ER*?

The revolving romances of *Grey's Anatomy*?

The never-ending chaos of *Chicago Hope*?

Now, see if it doesn't fit this simple formula –

Begin with the universally-shared vulnerability we all feel

about our personal health and well-being;

add in an uber-attractive cast wardrobed in

custom-fitted scrubs, intimidating white coats,

and some flattering back-lighting;

pepper the dialogue with just enough medical acronyms

and words that begin with 'hemo,' 'cardiac,' or 'thrombo'

to reach just beyond our layman's understanding;

mix in the drama of personal tragedies and broom

closet hook-ups, and what do you get?

The formula for a hit series with a devoted audience

that considers the lives of the fictitious characters

to be 'must-see' TV.

There's just something about the escapism of a good trauma drama.

On television.

From the comfort of our den couch.

However, in real life, short of celebrating the quick and trouble-free delivery of a newborn baby, there are few places *in the world* most of us would rather avoid more than a hospital—*especially the emergency room.*

But circling back to our multi-car highway accident, that's more than likely *exactly* where you would find yourself if you received any injuries of significance from the crash. That's because, once the call to 911 is made, your welfare becomes the responsibility of the sworn-to-serve first responders who arrive at the scene. They will stop the bleeding, take an initial assessment, and make the call whether you're going to the hospital or not. They will do what they have been trained to do in order to stabilize your situation and minimize further complications. *In the moment,* they literally assume control over your life because medical protocol demands it.

Like it or not, once they begin administering treatment, they make the calls—*all the calls*—about your welfare from the moment of their arrival up until the point when they hand you off to the doctors and nurses of the nearest emergency room.

Never mind that minutes before you may have been jamming out to a song on the radio or returning home from a great night out with friends or even just fighting rush hour traffic; *now you are at the mercy of others* for your well-being, *if not your very life.* To a considerably lesser degree, it's like this for a CMBS borrower who loses a major tenant. If a borrower reaches the point of requesting the intervention of their loan's Special Servicer, it is directly akin to calling 911 for urgent assistance. Though there may be no evidence of blood and guts spilled on the borrower's part, they are most certainly bleeding—*financially.* When a borrower's circumstances reach the point of notifying their Special Servicer, their *financial* well-being, *if not financial life,* is on the line.

It is also the time to seek outside counsel from

an experienced and qualified CMBS Borrower Advocate.

What many, many borrowers find out the very hard way is that CMBS restructuring is *not* for the uninitiated. There are twists and turns along the way most borrowers know nothing about. And *no one,* other than a highly experienced borrower advocate, will be forthcoming with the options and considerations available *for their benefit*. Without the input from a borrower advocate, most borrowers don't even know *what they don't know*.

Regrettably, most learn this fast and to their financial detriment.

Just as it is for the critically injured patient in the ambulance on the way to the hospital, it is for the unrepresented and ailing CMBS borrower: the people in charge don't have to explain what they're doing and don't have to give you options when survival is at risk; their job is to save what can be saved—*as it is, in its current state*. And what the people in charge are saving is the PROPERTY, not the borrower's investment.

That's probably why accident victims and distressed CMBS borrowers alike can both so readily identify with the *immediate invasiveness* they feel as soon as a call for help goes out.

If you've ever been taken by ambulance to your local hospital in an urgent situation, you know this to be true. No sooner are you handed off to the attending physician or nurse then your personal space absolutely ceases to exist. Whether you're conscious or not. Embarrassed or not. Or covered by insurance or not. Before you can tell them your name, who the current president is, or what year it is, it's likely your clothes have been torn open (if not removed), you've been given a mainline IV (to keep a vein accessible in the event of further complications), and you're being poked and prodded, examined and evaluated, in the time it takes you to give them your emergency contact information. And all of this is by a team of well-meaning, scrubbed up, gloved up *strangers*. Sure, they're licensed and educated and have seen it all before, but hey, you've never even met these people!

Assuming you're conscious and coherent, questions will come at you rapid fire. What medications are you taking? What's your medical and family history and, by the way, who is your insurance through? What happened that landed you there? All of this and lots more—*all at their complete and utter mercy*—and all as you lay partially undressed, dazed and confused, and in what is likely the worst pain of your life. To top it off, you've been momentarily relieved of your responsibility to make decisions for *yourself* regarding *your* health and welfare.

At this point, your options are clear and simple: lay there and accept the blood draws, scans, and treatment plans...or continue to suffer in your current state. It's the old 'take it or leave it' option in its most basic form.

And it's *very much* like this for the uninformed CMBS borrower when they request the intervention of the Special Servicer.

However, as I mentioned earlier, instead of arriving by ambulance, when a troubled CMBS borrower 'presents' by asking that their loan be transferred to the Special Servicer, they are making a serious concession. They are sending up a distress flag. Signaling the need for help. And usually out of other options.

The official name for this transfer of a CMBS loan *from* the management of the Master Servicer *to* the hopeful modifications of the Special Servicer occurs when a Letter of Imminent Default is sent. The Letter of Imminent Default is the industry standard whereby the borrower is officially putting its creditors on notice, signaling the likelihood (if not certainty) of trouble ahead. What this simply says is, "HELP! I may not be able to keep making timely payments on my loan now or in the near future without some assistance."

Maybe the claim is, "I didn't know my big box anchor tenant was moving out until last week," or "I've got several tenants suffering from a turndown in the market—they can't pay me so I can't pay you," or "I can't get a new loan sufficient to pay off my existing loan." Or one of a million other reasons.

Whatever the cause for the oncoming trouble, once the borrower issues the Letter of Imminent Default to their Master Servicer (again, akin to calling 911), there's a significant power shift—*from* the borrower *to* the Special Servicer and that's when the borrower becomes 'the patient.'

From this point on, the borrower's primary responsibility to the Special Servicer is to accommodate 'the new sheriff in town' as much as possible. If the Special Servicer tells the borrower to "jump," it can feel like the borrower's only option is to ask, "How high?"

Immediately upon the transfer of a loan from the Master Service to the Special Servicer, the Special Servicer becomes responsible for performing all types of reviews, much like when a patient is handed off from an EMT to an ER doc. Just as emergency personnel have to run a full battery of tests to understand an incoming patient's status, a Special Servicer has to have a clear understanding of what they're dealing with before they can begin to consider options to address the problem. From this point forward, the Special Servicer will make a full assessment of the property's current condition (as well as surrounding properties), identify areas of concern or those that need improvement (both immediately and long-term), and do a full study on the property's financial viability moving forward under current and projected market conditions.

It is likely a Special Servicer called into service will also request or personally perform the following:

» an appraisal on the property

» feedback from several trusted commercial real estate brokers based upon their reviews of the property, market conditions, potential options, and more

» possibly an environmental report depending upon past or current tenants that could have potentially affected the property's soil or even the nearby water table; dry cleaners are a prime example

» a personal, first-hand inspection (sometimes performed by an outside, paid company) to provide the most up-to-date and objective survey of the property's actual condition

Can you begin to see the parallels between our accident victim arriving at the ER and the call for help by a sinking CMBS borrower?

They're both extremely stressed.

It's likely neither personally knows the people ordering the tests, appraisals, and surveys on them or their property.

They're both being asked for (if not ordered to provide) answers and information that may have been private up to this point.

They are both likely in circumstances most definitely *not of their choosing.*

And they're both extremely concerned about how this will affect them moving forward.

It's no wonder that one of the most frequently used words by both ER patients and troubled commercial borrowers to describe their experiences is *intrusive.*

Sadly, oftentimes before a borrower fully understands the position they place themselves in by requesting a loan modification, it's too late to turn back. Just as an ER patient literally finds themselves laid bare with little say in their immediate treatment plan, once a troubled CMBS borrower sends up an urgent SOS, they too are basically laid bare and asked for the very thing they are usually lacking—cash. Typically, the *very first thing* a Special Servicer will ask of a borrower is, "What other money can you contribute as proof of your commitment to making good on any agreement we might reach?"

> Once a troubled CMBS borrower sends up an urgent SOS, they too are basically laid bare.

That's code for, "You need more 'skin in the game' if we're going to make this work."

And this is where the gravity of the situation frequently sets in for most troubled borrowers.

Common sense seems to dictate among most of us to stay afloat by our own means as long as possible. Fund until you can't anymore. Use every dollar available to you *before* giving even so much as a hint of possible trouble. *And this couldn't be more wrong for CMBS borrowers.*

It always, always, *always* behooves CMBS borrowers, when faced with *even an inkling* of concern regarding making their payments, to ask for assistance *sooner rather than later* and to *always* maintain a sizeable cash reserve for future negotiations with their Special Servicer. Otherwise, without *more money on the line,* a borrower's leverage in terms of accepting a Special Servicer's conditions is usually reduced to—you guess it—*take it or leave it.*

When a borrower is able and willing to make a further investment into a troubled property, they are making a strong case for supporting them. Anyone can say, "I want this to work. I believe this shortfall or these circumstances are temporary and fixable and I've got a plan for how to address them. Help me." But when a borrower arrives at the negotiating table, cash in hand, they are literally *putting their money where their mouth is.*

The next chapter will explain the motivations that affect how and why Special Servicers and Controlling Class Representatives

(CCRs) respond as they do to requests from borrowers facing financial difficulties. A thorough understanding of the payback structure that governs the whole CMBS process makes it much easier to understand *why* they do *what* they do. Special Servicers do, in fact, serve who they are appointed to serve. But to a struggling borrower, the realization that they're not at the top of the list is often one more hard-to-take blow to an already ailing outlook on their failing financial status.

It's also the time when those *most* committed to maintaining ownership of their property becomes most evident.

SPECIAL SERVICERS

THEIR MOTIVATION AND WHO
THEY *REALLY* SERVE

There's a reason the field of medicine is referred to as *a practice.*

It's dynamic and complicated. It's based upon centuries of research, yet changes continually. It involves painstaking precision and documentation of complex and *provable* data. And yet, somewhere in the midst of all that information and head knowledge, the human factor—with all its compassion and concern, sympathy and empathy—can't help but come into play in *the practice* of medicine.

And that's how it should be.

The treatment of another person's injury or illness, *if not their very life,* is a lot of responsibility to assume—even after more than a decade of intense and exhaustive training. Few people can appreciate this perspective more than emergency room doctors. They are notoriously well-schooled in triage protocol and come to learn almost intuitively how to prioritize immediate and life-saving care for their patients. Along the way, most also come to grasp the magnitude of what they do for a living. They know the decisions they are called on to make at a moment's notice aren't always easy or obvious. They know, in the heat of the moment, when a patient is begging for relief and emotions are off the charts, that the gravity of decisions made *today* can affect their patients for rest of their lives.

Not only is it a mind-numbing responsibility to treat the sick and suffering *and* to fully understand the mechanics of the human body, but *every single patient presents differently.* That means every single patient a doctor encounters shows up with more than just symptoms and injuries. They also bring with them their own set of quirks and qualms and fears and worries and no two are the same. *And they're never more evident than in emergency situations.* One patient might have an extremely low pain tolerance while another hardly flinches even with a bone exposed. One shows up completely coherent and ready to share her full life's history and the passenger in the same accident can't remember their address. One is compliant and receptive to treatment just as another is refusing everything and calling his lawyer to threaten malpractice. All types show up.

Life in a big city ER is crazy, chaotic, and completely unpredictable, to say the least. And just for good measure, and to complicate the whole trauma protocol *even more,* the patients with the most severe injuries, *especially the kinds received from a serious automobile crash,* almost always require a whole range of treatments.

Multiple injuries call for *multiple* specialists.

Multiple specialists bring with them *multiple* opinions.

Multiple opinions inevitably give way to *multiple* temperaments, professional tendencies, and broad reaching levels of experience.

. But what happens when those called in for consultations and opinions arrive at different conclusions and suggest different treatment plans even when given access *to the exact same test results, scans, and other evaluations?* Who's right? What if Dr. Jackson believes surgery is the best treatment while Dr. Miller prefers a less invasive approach? Both believe their treatment plan is the best; both can make a solid case for why theirs is the preferred; and both are working towards the same end; they're just proposing different methods of arriving there.

When a Special Servicer is called upon in a distressed situation, they also have 'treatment' options for dealing with a distressed borrower. Their process is also dynamic and complicated. It's based upon decades of research, yet changes continually. It involves painstaking precision and documentation of complex and *provable* data and no two situations are alike. There are also many specialists involved in the ultimate decision-making process (appraisers, environmental consultants, brokers, lawyers to name a few). The biggest difference, however, between the traditional doctor-patient relationship and the Special Servicer-troubled borrower relationship all comes down to *who serves whom.* It's also one of the biggest causes of further frustration, misunderstanding, and financial pain for an already-ailing borrower.

Here's why:

Borrowers who are hurting financially

and who have asked for help

incorrectly assume they are *the patient* in the relationship;

however, as far as the Special Servicer is concerned,

the only *'patients'* they are responsible for serving

are the bond certificate holders whose investments

funded the loan in the first place.

Even if a Special Servicer empathizes with the circumstances and considers them regretful, possibly even out of the borrower's control, they are still charged with one straightforward task—to maximize the recovery of, and minimize the losses to, the investments of certificate holders of the CMBS pool they represent.

The options for accommodations and modifications available to a Special Servicer *for the collective welfare of the investors* are governed by the Servicing Standards established in the Pooling and Servicing Agreement (PSA). The PSA is a case-specific document which clearly identifies the expectations and requirements of the Special Servicer and it is not accessible to a borrower. It establishes the hierarchy of repayment schedules based upon bond classes and sets the boundaries for what a Special Servicer can and cannot do in an effort to receive the greatest return on investment on a CMBS property. Everything a Special Servicer does is governed by this obligation—*with no regard to the borrower's financial welfare*. In fact, *what the borrower wants* is not even factored into the equation at all.

In fact, what the borrower wants is not even factored into the equation at all.

And it gets even more complicated when you add the ultimate decision maker, the Controlling Class Representative (CCR) for the particular pool the loan is in, to the mix. As the representative of the lowest rated investors and therefore those at the highest risk of loss on their investment, each CCR has its own motivations, financial implications, and decision-making protocol. Yet a borrower will never speak to a CCR, and in most cases, won't even know about the CCR, let alone know their identity.

This is also the turning point at which a borrower usually realizes they're not just in over their head *financially*, but *contractually* as well. Without the guidance of an experienced borrower advocate—literally, someone who has 'been there, done that,' many times over—a drowning borrower may not ever receive the life-preserving option they are so desperately seeking.

The game is rigged.

The game is rigged.

The cards are stacked against them.

And the forecast is dismal. This is the point where most borrowers finally come to understand and accept they 'don't even know what they don't know.'

But why now?

Because they've reached the point of needing help; because they've since realized the person they *correctly* turned to for help is accountable *to someone else*; and shockingly, because the one they once *thought* was supposed to help them, won't even tell them what options are available.

You read that right—

> A Special Servicer is under *no obligation*
>
> to identify what they can and cannot do
>
> to help a struggling CMBS borrower and
>
> they usually don't.

So, who is looking out for the borrower in all of this?

Consider the absurdity of this equation in another setting: You're out and about running errands and get hungry. You see a sign that says 'In & Out' and it looks to be a fast food drive-thru restaurant. Most of us know the bright yellow arrow and the 'In & Out' logo to mean crazy good burgers fixed just the way we like them, but let's assume you're new to town and unfamiliar with the burger chain.

You pull up to the drive-thru window and notice the menu is missing but go ahead and order a basic salad. "I'm sorry, ma'am, we don't serve salads," comes the voice from the black box. "What else would you like?"

"No worries," you say. "How about a bowl of soup?"

"We don't serve soup, either. What else would you like?"

"Hmmmm...I guess I'll just settle for three tacos, please."

"We don't serve tacos, either. What else..."

"So you're a fast food place. You can't make me a salad. You don't serve soup. And I can't even get an order of tacos. What is it that you can give me?"

"What would you like, ma'am?"

And so it goes. You've arrived with a felt need—a growling stomach—and a ready solution. They can't or won't provide what you've asked for—a salad, soup, or tacos—but they continue to ask what it is you'd like. Before your head explodes in frustration, you can't help but wonder, "Wouldn't this have been a million times easier if they'd just tell me *what they can offer me?*"

Sure it would have been easier *for you.* But they don't have to—they're In & Out Burgers. They have a cult following. They have secret menu for the uber-well-informed. They serve who they serve so well, they don't have to indulge the uneducated because they figure, if you really want to know what they're all about, you'll talk to somebody who already knows a lot about them.

Now, imagine a similar conversation as a patient in the emergency room. You show up with what you think to be a broken arm and the conversation goes something like this:

"Yes, sir…how can we help you?"

"Well, I'm pretty sure my arm is broken."

"What would like me to do?"

"Well, I'm no doctor, but I was thinking maybe an x-ray and a cast would be in order."

"I'm sorry, sir, but I'm unable to do that for you. What else would you like me to do?" And this is where it gets beyond baffling.

You've shown up to a large metropolitan emergency room, doctors, nurses, techs, and gurneys are *everywhere*. There's a gunshot wound in the bay to your left, an elderly Alzheimer's patient to your right, and all you're asking for is a quick x-ray and a simple cast. But what you don't know, is that the receptionist honestly can't x-ray your arm or put you in a cast. She can direct you to a bed, file your paperwork, and request a physician consult, but she doesn't offer any of those.

All she asks is what she is obligated to ask, "What would you like me to do?"

See how it works? You don't know what to ask for, so you don't get the help you're wanting and needing. You're hurting and frustrated and angry because *you didn't know what you didn't know.*

Welcome to life as an uninformed and ailing CMBS borrower.

Remember, because CMBS loans are non-recourse, the only collateral available to service the loan is the actual property itself; the owners are not held personally liable for the repayment of the debt. As a result, in a default situation, the Special Servicer is presented with only two possible scenarios—foreclosure and sale of the property *or* reach an agreement with the borrower regarding repayment terms. For a Special Servicer to even consider agreeing to the repayment terms, the borrower has to offer a structure that will be better for the certificate holders than if the special servicer foreclosed and ultimately sold the property (based on the Special Servicer's opinion).

But how is a borrower to even know what is on the menu of this Special Servicer *for this specific pool?* How do they know what best to offer for the highest chance of approval? How do they *begin to know* what specifics a Special Servicer is requiring even to consider making any accommodations?

Start with money; follow with a plan.

For CMBS borrowers requesting loan modifications, assistance is available, but it can come at a tremendous expense. Once a borrower reaches the distress stage, it usually takes a substantial offering of new capital *on their part* to motivate a Special Servicer to even discuss making any allowances. For a struggling borrower dealing with the angst of insufficient funds, compounded by the request for *more money,* (and usually the inability to offer none), this is akin to adding salt to a massive wound. Hurt upon hurt… down and close to out…and needing the very thing that's required of them just to keep going and save their investment. And then the questions settle in--*How much* additional money do I have to put into the property?

How long it will take to stabilize the property? Do market forecasts look hopeful or are downturns expected?

Will the property even bring *the original investment?* If not, what will it take to reach that point?

What are the chances I'll get my *'new money'* out of the property?

Besides all the speculations and assumptions about their property's potential, borrower's also have to ask themselves if they even have it 'in them' to invest further time, money, and effort into something *with a decidedly uncertain outcome* to make it worth it to them?

For the troubled CMBS borrower,

sometimes it boils down to a matter of selecting

the 'best' of the bad options available to them.

Medically speaking, this might be comparable to someone receiving a terminal diagnosis and facing the decision whether to undergo the brutality of chemo or other radical measures or to forgo further treatment and live their remaining time free of medical intervention. A borrower facing the uphill climb of recovering a depleted cash reserve or negative cash flow must also decide if the fight to maintain their investment is worth the struggle.

As legitimate as the borrower's concerns are to them personally, it is still the opinion of the Special Servicer and ultimately the CCR that decides which resolution path is chosen. They, too, have to answer some very difficult questions and consider lots of unknowns before ultimately selecting what they consider to be *the best of the bad* options available *to them.* This usually involves taking many factors into consideration including –

--market conditions and the property's presumed potential

--the borrower's willingness to work towards an agreement by providing 'more skin in the game' in the form of new capital

--the Special Servicer's own investment in the CMBS pool

No doubt, those involved on both sides of a CMBS agreement must answer some tough questions before requesting or granting any type of accommodation. So many variables to consider. Hard and fast rules and restrictions come up alongside gray areas open to interpretation and perspective and experience. Personal temperaments and tendencies add to the unpredictability. Especially from a borrower's point of view, navigating the twists and turns that come with seeking accommodations on a failing CMBS loan can literally seem all but impossible.

But help is worth seeking. Though it be painful, it is better than *not seeking any help.* Besides, *the right kind of help* is invaluable.

It can save your financial life.

It can breathe new life into you.

It can enable you, strengthen you, and come alongside of you to fight another battle.

7

THE GOLDEN HOUR, THE PLATINUM 10, AND THE NEED FOR SPEED

R ush Hour traffic is a beating anyway you look at it. You're gearing up for the day ahead or winding down from the one you just had. You want to *already* be where you want *to be* and not bother with all the other bozos gunning for the same thing. It doesn't matter if you're trying to make it to Family Burger Night, Happy Hour with friends, or a quiet evening alone with a pizza and the sole control of the remote, *we all want to get to where we want to go as fast as possible.* Problem is, so does the guy in the '97

Corolla beside you…and the fleet of 18-wheelers coming up behind you trying to make their destination on time…and the lady in front of you who's been riding her brake the last five miles. Everybody is thinking the same thing:

How fast can I get to where I want to be?

This means we go a little faster than usual, maybe take a few more chances than normal, and usually get a bit more aggressive and less gracious when it comes to other drivers. It also means we increase the chances for being involved in or causing a serious automobile accident, too. For the first responders that show up for the accidents that inevitably ensue *for someone*, time matters *tremendously* to them as well.

Time matters *to them* because if you're seriously injured in a multi-vehicle wreck, time matters *to you*.

Especially the first hour.

Which probably explains why it's called *the Golden Hour*—the highly precious, highly important, first 60 minutes following any type of traumatic physical injury—especially those received in high-impact car crashes. Decades of well-documented evidence backed by battlefield tactics and countless ER patients makes an undeniable case for treatment within the Golden Hour and the life-and-death difference it can make.

THE GOLDEN HOUR, THE PLATINUM 10, AND THE NEED FOR SPEED

Originally credited to Dr. R. Adams Cowley, a military surgeon who put his wartime practices to use once he returned to private practice, Cowley explained the urgency for treatment this way:

> "There is a golden hour between life and death. If
> you are critically injured,
> you have less than 60 minutes to survive. You might
> not die right then;
> it may be three days or two weeks later—
> but something has happened in your body that
> is irreparable."[3]

Those are powerful words coming from the man who eventually came to be known as the 'Father of Trauma Medicine' and head of the University of Maryland Shock Trauma Center that also bears his name. But Cowley's principles and practices go well beyond just the basic preservation of life. Saving a patient's life through urgent evaluation and treatment is the obvious first step; but response to and proper treatment of massive injuries within the Golden Hour brings with it a lifetime of implications as well. Issues such as a patient's quality of life going forward, the length of their hospital stay, the possibility of crushing medical bills, and the potential drain on medical resources and personnel are all *very real* considerations that support Cowley's simple premise—*taking action as soon as trouble happens matters now and later.*

In recent years, many EMTs have come to take Cowley's practices a step further, practicing what they now refer to as the **Platinum 10**—the *very first* 10 minutes once they arrive at the scene. The goal of the Platinum 10 is to focus intently on initial patient assessment, emergency stabilization, patient packaging, and initiation of transport. In other words, determine what needs to be done, do it, and get moving—*fast.*

There's an old saying that says, "All bleeding eventually stops." It's true, but there's really only one preferable outcome if survival is your goal. The bleeding can stop due to treatment from specially trained and experienced professionals or you can simply bleed out. Not much of a decision, is it?

Time and timely treatment can also matter even if your injuries aren't life-threatening. Consider an injury that is simpler, much less urgent. Even if it is something as minor as a broken arm, waiting can be catastrophic. Here's how: You feel the snap in your forearm and your wrist goes limp—all the classic signs of a break. *But,* you've got an extremely high insurance deductible which means the first $10,000 is all yours before insurance takes over. You do a quick review of finances in your head and decide you just can't afford to have it looked at immediately and decide to power through the pain for as long as you can.

THE GOLDEN HOUR, THE PLATINUM 10, AND THE NEED FOR SPEED

You make a trip to the drug store, grab a basic splint and wrap it up tight to fortify your useless limb. The Tylenol you took the first day is wearing thin as the pain continues to increase, so you double-down and start taking ibuprofen between doses. You live the longest week and a half of your life in complete pain.

"I can't go on like this," you finally concede and head to the closest urgent care clinic. You rationalize it has to be cheaper than going to a mega-hospital because, really, what difference does it make who shoots an x-ray of your arm and slaps on a simple cast?

The on-call clinic doctor is one year out of med school and used to treating mainly sinus infections and kids' colds. Still, he confirms your arm is seriously broken and that you have a full-scale complex fracture that is best treated by an orthopedic specialist. He resplints your arm with his medical grade version and writes out the referral info and a prescription for two weeks of stronger pain relief. You bought yourself some time, but now you'll face both bills—his and the specialist's.

Even though you sparse out the pain pills for an entire month, the pain remains and the swelling won't seem to go away. You get an appointment with the orthopedic doc for the next day and your prognosis goes from bad to worse. When she tells you your ligaments and tendons are damaged as well as the broken arm, surgery is what she considers to be the strongest preference followed by an extensive treatment plan and lengthy rehabilitation just to return to functionality. She doesn't give you the option of thinking about it for several months while you save to meet your deductible. Waiting will only make a bad situation worse. Waiting will give the bone an opportunity to heal—misaligned or possibly deformed. And by the way, she has this Thursday at 9:00 a.m. open for surgery.

> Golden Hour—the highly precious, highly important, first 60 minutes following any type of traumatic physical injury.

And this all happens *because you waited to ask for help.*

Now you realize—what could have been a simple fix grew worse, not better, over time. You tried to handle the discomfort on your own but have abruptly just run out of options. Now it's going to be a much more extensive process, cost you much, much more, and be a very painful road back to complete functionality.

Lesson learned. Making a decision, accepting treatment, bearing the temporary pain is ten-fold preferable to denying the problem, delaying treatment, and opening the door to potentially and most certainly, unnecessary further complications.

The same principle is true for borrowers faced with the probability of not being able to continue making their monthly payments on a timely basis. Time matters. The sooner a distressed borrower requests the intervention of the Special Servicer, the better the resolution options available to them. Not only is it *highly desirable* for a potentially troubled borrower to solicit help from their Special Servicer, it is *equally imperative* for this borrower to *fully understand* the options available to them followed up by their submission of their *ultimate desired request* within 90 days.

In the world of CMBS servicing,
90 days is the Golden Hour.
The longer a loan is in Special Servicing without
a formal request from the borrower, the higher the
likelihood the property will be foreclosed on.

Remember, the Special Servicer is primarily concerned with servicing the investors, not the borrower, and more often than not, they take action well within the 90-day Golden Hour period—and it is usually to the borrower's detriment. The sooner a borrower comes forward with a suggested resolution plan, the much greater their chances of receiving acceptable accommodations to save their loan. In other words, borrowers who *ask early* and *ask specifically* are always more successful in retaining their property.

The paradox to this borrower/Special Servicer equation
is that timeliness is primarily a one-way street.

For borrowers, it is imperative that they *act* and *ask* as soon as challenges arise. For Special Servicers, the process of modifying a CMBS loan can take a year or more. Much of this is due to the fact that Special Servicers are the multi-taskers within the CMBS ranks. They have options and proposals to consider, outside consultants and contractors busy preparing and submitting their analyses, recommendations, and anticipated expenses, the back-and-forth of negotiations with other parties, and lots of legalese involved. All this just to service *one* CMBS loan from a workload of several!

To better understand how this whole hurry-up-and-wait game plays out, here is a typical timeline of the CMBS loan modification process –

Months 1 & 2 –

The borrower makes their '911 call' to their Master Servicer and makes the formal request for their loan to be transferred to the Special Servicer; this transfer can take up to 60 days;

Month 3 –

Immediately upon landing at the Special Servicer, the Special Servicer begins ordering all the 'tests' on the property to understand the situation, the current market, and the future value of the property. *This* is the Golden Hour for borrowers. The first 90 days are the most critical and important timeframe for borrowers to present a sound proposal to the Special Servicer. This is because, without a well-thought out plan submitted from the borrower, the Special Servicer will come up with its own idea of how to resolve the situation and it likely will include them taking the property back via foreclosure.

And remember—a borrower will not be provided with a menu of possible options for resolution which means they *already need to know* what is even available for consideration by the Special Servicer and CCR based upon the precise terms of their original loan agreement. That's why a borrower advocate is so critical to the process.

Months 4 & 5 –

The Special Servicer reviews all the information, including any proposal submitted by the borrower, and will likely start to give feedback about the resolution.

Month 6 –9

Negotiations take place between the borrower and the Special Servicer for the purpose of coming up with a resolution that meets the objectives of the Special Servicer, the CCR, and hopefully, the borrower.

Months 9 - 12 –

When negotiations are complete and deal terms are agreed to, the legal process is started and modification documents are drafted and finalized.

Finally –

The deal closes!

It takes a lot of perseverance on everyone's part to see this process through to the end. The temptation for a borrower to give up hope and walk away from their property is always present. One more study, one more analysis, one more challenge can wear down a weary borrower's gumption to see the changes through til the end.

A troubled CMBS borrower is every bit a trauma patient with the potential to bleed out *of cash* if assistance doesn't come quick enough and with the proper means to stop the bleeding. They come to the table with lots of stress, possibly regret, and usually fear for what lies ahead.

But their call to me for help is a sure sign they haven't given up yet.

A DEEPER DIVE INTO THE OPTIONS

Unexpected and sometimes tragic events have a way of reminding us *not everything is in our control.* Even the most independent among us occasionally find ourselves in situations we couldn't have anticipated or prepared for *no matter what.* That's almost always the case for injured ER patients and distressed CMBS borrowers—*neither* of them intentionally meant to end up where they are.

No one gets in their car expecting to get hit by a swerving 18-wheeler. Most of us are more concerned with what we're going to order when we get to the restaurant or how the report we just sent will go over with the boss. Nobody turns the key thinking, "Next stop—City General ER."

But things happen. Unforeseen, unpredictable, *unavoidable* events come out of nowhere and can land a driver in a world of serious pain.

It happens to CMBS borrowers, too.

No borrower enters into such an arrangement with plans to default on their loan or deal with broken leases and bankrupt tenants. No one intentionally plans to fall short. But things happen—unforeseen, unpredictable, *unavoidable...*

> No borrower enters into such an arrangement with plans to default.

When accommodations are needed, these are the four primary options available to CMBS borrowers *and* Special Servicers and they range from relatively minor accommodations to an all-out 'get out of jail free' pass. Though they fall into one of only four categories, the modifications that can be made, the exceptions that can be considered, and the constraints that are subject to discretion are virtually *endless* depending upon the specifics of every unique CMBS borrower, the loan documents, and its servicers.

4 Traditional Options; Endless Arrangements –

Each of the following examples are taken from real-life comparable experiences I've had with clients. If there is a take-away from these examples for CMBS borrowers, I would offer it is two-fold: the first and most obvious is to be prepared—*perpetually prepared* as much as is possible; and the equally important second take-away reminds me of an old, but so appropriate adage—'the devil is in the details.' Borrowers that honor these two lessons may never find themselves in need of loan modifications but for those who do, they have a much greater probability of maintaining ownership of their commercial property *and* their financial standing.

Maturity date extension –

This is usually the simplest request and would only apply for a borrower that has a maturity loan and just needs a little time to pay it off.

Let's assume a borrower has a 10-year, $30 million CMBS loan that matures in a little over three months. Currently, the property is performing well and the borrower has plenty of equity in it. Realizing the maturity date is fast approaching, the borrower begins the refinancing process 90 days in advance. Everything goes smoothly during the refinancing process and his processor sets a closing date set for the same date as the CMBS loan's expiration date. One loan will mature; a new one fund. The transfer of funding is set to happen virtually simultaneously.

However, when the new lender hits a snag and funding is delayed *by one week only,* the borrower thinks, "What's the big deal with a week? I'm sure my old lender will cut me some slack. What's to worry about?"

A lot.

A $1.5 million late fee on his payoff statement *is what to worry about.*

Calls are made. Explanations are given. Pleas are presented.

"What the...? I thought you guys knew I had done everything I could to make this happen on time. I had everything all lined up. I made sure everything was set; that my new financing was scheduled to close *the exact same day* as my loan with you all was due. I can't help it if some junior servicing guy in a branch office gets behind on his paperwork and delays the funding for a week! Give a guy a break! All these years of never missing a payment and growing a great property and this is how you treat me? You gotta be kidding!"

Unfortunately for the borrower, good intentions and a flawless payment history don't get you too far when you've signed a binding contract that clearly identifies the penalties for late payments. In this case, the hefty late payment penalty stuck because it was allowed for in the contract language. What this borrower learned, the very hard and expensive way, was that many CMBS servicers charge a 5% late fee on a balloon payment (in this case it was $30 million). Unless the CMBS loan documents specifically exclude the balloon payment from the late fee definition, borrowers are subject to the full 5% fee *even if they are just days late* making their final payment.

Had the borrower realized this, he could have reached out to the Special Servicer *prior to* the maturity date to request a *formal forbearance* of the maturity date by 30 days and completely avoided the stiff penalty.

Many CMBS servicers charge a 5% late fee on a balloon payment (in this case it was $30 million).

Payment modification –

This is probably the most widely used form of accommodation for a struggling CMBS borrower because the trigger event that pitches them into distress is frequently curable within the remainder of the term of the loan, so it is a temporary 'income' issue only.

In this case, let's assume a borrower has a $20 million CMBS loan on a property with Toys R Us as one of the major tenants. He hears rumors of trouble for the giant toy retailer and keeps an eye on store activity and financials, but still remains confident in the chain's long-term retail presence across the country.

Until the sudden announcement that Toys R Us plans to close all of its stores. Every. Single. One of them.

The borrower makes the calls, arranges showings of the soon-to-be vacant megastore, and courts potential clients feverishly. Cautious relief sets in when a prospect shows interest in the space. "The wheels are in motion," he thinks. "We'll get TRU out, bring it back to life with a few improvements, and be good as gold."

And then he comes to better understand the 'double hit' to revenue and expenses that can occur with an unexpected vacancy of this size. His new tenant improvement costs (from the only interested prospect) well exceed his estimates when the two-month renovation project becomes four months. So now, not only is no revenue currently coming in from the huge vacancy left by Toys R Us, but the borrower is spending considerably more than he had planned for to accommodate the prospective new tenant. At this rate, it isn't long before these two factors become too much and he falls behind to the point of defaulting on her loan.

Looking back, it's easy to arm-chair quarterback what went wrong. Because he mistakenly believed his troubles were over once he had a replacement tenant lined up, he failed to take into account *all the other things* that could affect the cash flow. Even though he had funds on reserve for tenant improvements, he hadn't also figured in delays in finish out and an extended time without income from the large space.

When his reserves began to plummet, he calls his Special Servicer (assuming he had thought ahead and had his loan transferred from Master Servicer to Special Servicer at the time Toys R Us announced its closing) to let him know the status of things. Rather than offering a hearty congratulations for landing another large tenant so soon, the first thing the Special Servicer asked the borrower was, "What *new* money are you *personally* going to contribute towards the situation?"

"*More* money? *New* money? Don't you think I've used everything I've got to keep this property afloat?" he demanded. "I landed the tenant—and that was not an easy find considering the size of the vacancy left behind. I've gone through my reserves for tenant improvements in the first two months, and if I had *more* money or *new* money, I wouldn't be calling you now!"

Not only is the Special Servicer less than sympathetic with the troubled borrower, but they also threaten foreclosure on the loan. When the borrower's new tenant learns of the potential default, they become 'spooked' and opt for another location. At this point, the borrower is out of options and the Special Servicer forecloses on the property, causing the borrower to lose everything he had invested in it.

Had this *same* borrower, when faced with the *same* circumstances, made a call *before he ran out of funds*, he could have requested the loan be transferred to the Special Servicer *immediately* and capitalized on the tremendous value of acting proactively within the Golden Hour. And had he consulted with a borrower advocate, he also would have known to submit a thorough and well thought out plan in writing to the Special Servicer within 30 days of the loan being transferred. In this proposal, it would have been entirely appropriate to request future loan payments be immediately reduced as well as all net cash flow to be placed into a designated reserve account dedicated solely to tenant improvements for the new tenant. The borrower would have then had the freedom to execute the new tenant's terms for improvements without fear of penalties or even foreclosure once the space was complete. Once the new tenant was in place and was making monthly payments, the borrower could have then requested the note be transferred back to the original Master Servicer.

Debt deferral –

As the landscape of retail shopping continues to move toward online buying, this 'option' is being considered in an increasing number of situations.

Now let's consider a borrower with an $80 million CMBS loan on a mall that matures in 2022. Unfortunately for him, many of the anchor tenants have left and moved to the newer, more popular town center-type of shopping areas. When the loan was originated, the property's value was over $100 million, but the vacancies have resulted in a dramatic drop in value—to $50 million. The borrower has done his best to cover the loss of rent income for as long as he can, but when his funds run out, he has no other choice but to default on his payment.

At this point, his loan is transferred to the Special Servicer who begins making their own assessments of the property's current value. They also conclude that the property is worth $50 million and that it would also cost *at least* $25 million to stabilize it and turn it back into a well-performing mall.

Because of such a significant drop in valuation and the need for another $25 million of capital, the borrower is not sure what his options were, so he asks the Special Servicer for the 'menu of his options.' The Special Servicer, much like the order taker at In-and-Out, tells the borrower that he can't and won't provide a menu of accommodations possibly available to the him. The borrower is left to try and figure out what would work on his own. With no understanding of his available options, this borrower asks for a temporary reduction in payments

The borrower is left to try and figure out what would work on his own.

so he can keep the loan current while he works to stabilize and transform the property. The Special Servicer quickly agrees to this plan because it is in *their best interest* and because every dollar spent by the borrower will ultimately work to increase the property's value. This is all in the Special Servicer and investors' best interest! It also allows for the loan to remain current with no loss to the certificate holders since the borrower doesn't know to request any reduction or deferral in the principal balance.

Under the conditions granted, things go well for the borrower *for a while*. Things are good until they are not.

He is able to keep the loan current, put an *additional* $25 million into the property (as promised), and is very close to stabilizing the property...*until his 2022 maturity comes due* and he realizes he is running out of time and is still not in a position to make full repayment. His property value is now $70 million, but not the $80 million he owes.

The borrower then requests a 3-year extension of the maturity date to allow time for the property to further stabilize—hopefully to the point of refinancing and paying off the original $80 million debt. He is sure the Special Servicer will be happy to accommodate, especially since he was so accommodating to him last time and he has now put $25 million more into the property. But this time, the Special Servicer is not as accommodating. He denies the request and demands that the loan be paid off upon the maturity date. Sadly, because the borrower is unable to find new financing sufficient to pay off the $80 million, the loan falls into a maturity default and the Special Servicer forecloses on the property, leaving the borrower to suffer not only the loss of the property, but also *all* of the *additional* $25 million he has invested during the stabilization period.

The Special Servicer and the certificate holders were all too happy with this outcome!

The outcome could have been much more favorable though for the borrower if he knew the menu of options.

Assuming the same conditions for the distressed mall ($80 million original note, $50 million current valuation, $25 million for renovation), the borrower should have (a) requested his loan be transferred to the Special Servicer *as soon as* his cash flow was not sufficient to cover his loan payments (not when he ran out of funds), (b) *not* continued to come out of pocket to keep the loan current (but rather kept the funds available as "new skin in the game" to make a deal with the Special Servicer), and (c) understood his menu of options. Had he also understood the full benefit of the Golden Hour, he could have benefitted from his timely action. He could have then submitted his plans to stabilize the property, by asking for a 'debt deferral' which works something like this:

Bifurcate (divide in two) the loan –

»   An 'A note' equal to $50 million (the appraised value of the property). The new payments would be made only on the $50 million note .

»   A 'B note' (or hope note) equal to $30 million, or the difference between the 'A Note' and the total loan balance ($80 million minus $50 million). It's called a hope note because there are no payments due on it and it is there in HOPES that the property value will increase.

»   Borrower contributes $25 million of new equity, which is then used to stabilize the property.

  o   The loan's maturity date is extended to 2025 to allow sufficient time to stabilize.

Upon maturity, the loan is to be repaid in the following order:

1.   Repayment of the $50 million 'A note' in full

2.   Borrower receives his $25 million of new equity

3. Any remaining proceeds would then be split between the borrower and the pay down of the 'B Note'/hope note

4. Any remaining balance owed on the 'B Note'/hope note is then written off

These vastly different outcomes for the *exact same set of circumstances* highlight the importance of **knowing your options and seeking help early.**

Debt forgiveness –

This is the most severe resolution for all the parties involved as this means funds are sacrificed for the sake of saving a property from total foreclosure and/or abandonment.

Let's take our same borrower as above under the same dire circumstances, making the same poor decision to use all his funds for as long as he can before finally defaulting on the loan. Again, the Special Servicer takes over the management of the loan and makes their usual assessments. But this time, not only do they confirm the property is worth approximately $50 million and needing an additional $25 million to make it somewhat viable, they also conclude that the mall *will likely never be worth the $80 million (the loan balance) again in the near future!*

The borrower reluctantly agrees that the property has likely been permanently over-leveraged and that the value will likely never get to $100 million (the original value of the property) again in his own lifetime. Again, because he is unaware of the menu of options available to him, he asks the Special Servicer for a *reduction in payments only* so he can keep the loan current while working to find a long-term solution. In his mind, he is taking comfort in believing he is a 'good borrower' because he is actively trying to raise the property's value by contributing an additional $25 million in updates and improvements. Because of this, he makes the *very wrong* assumption that his Special Servicer will work with him once the loan matures.

Needless to say, the Special Servicer gladly welcomes this plan because it means no loss today to the investors and possibly even less loss later on,

Under the first possible outcome, the capital investment of $25 million, will greatly increase the attractiveness of the property to the point where many of the vacancies can probably be filled, the borrower can continue making payments over the life of the loan, and the balance can be paid in full upon the loan's maturity date.

The second alternative is still more beneficial for the investors than an *immediate* loss, *but not so much for the borrower*. When the borrower is granted the reduction in payments, he is then able to make his monthly payments all the way to the loan's maturity date. He invests the extra $25 million into improving the property in hopes of increasing its value and attractiveness to potential tenants. And through it all, he still believes his consistent track history regarding making payments and his good faith measure of the additional investment will be taken into consideration should he need a bit of debt forgiveness when the loan reaches the maturity date.

However, when the appraisals are done near the maturity date and the total debt owed is still much greater than its value, the borrower takes what he believes to be the next logical step: a request for partial debt forgiveness. But when the Special Servicer denies his request and demands the loan be paid *in full* off upon reaching the maturity date, the borrower is finally forced to concede to the worst-case outcome: maturity default. Soon thereafter, the Special Servicer forecloses on the property and again the borrower loses his investment in the property *plus* all of the additional $25 million he put into the property during the stabilization period.

The borrower could have saved himself a tremendous amount of time, effort, and money if he had known to request a *discounted payoff* of the note *before* he emptied his cash reserves completely and *before* he somehow managed to put an additional $25 million into the mall. When the updated appraisal of $50 million confirmed the property's plummeting value and with all other variables giving little

There were
many other
options
available to
this borrower
if only he had
a menu!

hope to ever even reaching the original $80 million loan amount, he would have been wise to know his available options and cut his losses as if his financial life depended on it—*because it quite literally did.* There were many other options available to this borrower if only he had a menu!

As we've discussed, there's a lot on the line with commercial real estate investments, even under ideal circumstances. But the stakes go up when an 'accident happens.'

CMBS loans—*for borrowers and investors*— are just like any other financial investment--the outcomes can *and will* vary depending on which side of the equation you're on, the return is never guaranteed, and the success-failure spectrum can run quite a broad gamut. On all levels and under all circumstances—known, anticipated, or completely unforeseeable—CMBS loans present both an opportunity *and* a risk for everyone involved.

But then, so does driving home from work every day in rush hour traffic.

A NOTE FROM THE AUTHOR

Helpful

Informative

Insightful

These were my goals when I first undertook this book. I wanted to take the complicated and sometimes mysterious Commercial Mortgage Backed Securities industry and demystify it. Identify who was responsible for doing what, when, how, and mostly WHY.

Sounds simple enough, right?

Classic case of 'easier said than done.'

If there's one common theme throughout the book I hope you grasped, this is —*every CMBS transaction is unique.* No two transactions are *ever* precisely alike. The people, the properties, the terms—something, *if not many things*—will always differ from one transaction to another. No standard template, flowchart, or one-size-fits-all plan is ever the case. It's simply a byproduct of what it is—a highly structured arrangement between a borrower and many 'lenders,' all governed by the Securities and Exchange Commission (SEC) and the Internal Revenue Service (IRS). Add to this the fact that the 'lenders' are, for the most part, unidentifiable bond holders seeking a return on their investment. You are borrowing from people you don't know and others are lending to people *they* don't know—*you*.

This is not your father's bank loan!

Keep in mind that the many examples, illustrations, and case studies in these chapters are literally just the tip of the iceberg for the options and opportunities available to both servicers and borrowers that can accompany every CMBS arrangement. And that, my friends, is what the next book is for.

ENDNOTES

[1]Johnson, Allie. "When You Should—and Shouldn't—Call 911." SafeBee.com, SafeBee, April 21, 2015, http://www.safebee.com/home/when-you-should-and-shouldnt-call-911.

[2]McKeon, Price. "HSPD: Accidental 911 Call by Criminal Leads Them to Him." Fox16.com, Nexstar Media Group, Inc., October 8, 2018, https://www.fox16.com/crime/hspd-accidental-911-call-by-criminal-leads-them-to-him/1508068728.

[3]"History of the Shock Trauma Center - Tribute to R. Adams Cowley, MD." UMMS.org, University of Maryland Medical Center, https://www.umms.org/ummc/health-services/shock-trauma/about/history.

For more information about CMBS and Ann Hambly visit:

1STSSS.COM